*The Best of Natural Eating
Around the World*

The Best of Natural Eating
Around the World

ELIZABETH ALSTON

FOOD EDITOR

Redbook MAGAZINE

David McKay Company, Inc.

NEW YORK

This book is for everyone who feeds himself or a family, every day, in hope that it will make that tremendous task a little bit easier and a lot more fun.

Thank you, Dick Lansing, for help way beyond husbandly love, for being the advocate for clarity, and a discerning taster. Thank you, Dr. Jean Mayer, for reading the introduction. I have learned much from working with you. Thank you, Christiana Lindsay Sutor, and Richard, too, for working on the grain chapter, and much more. Thank you, Judy Broudy, for helping with research and assembling the mail-order list. Thank you, Dionis Lindsay, Risa Firestone, Willie Mae Hudson, and Susanna Goldman, for helping shop, test, and clean up.

Contents

Introduction

I was not nurtured in the lap of *haute cuisine.*

True, life got off to a good start on mother's milk. Next came "Cow and Gate" formula, minced (cooked ground) beef, mashed potatoes, stewed apples, and custard-from-a-mix. My first brush with French food came when I was around six and Miss Polly Underwood started her French language class by taking her students into her kitchen and staging a tea party: *"le thé, du lait, le tartine, le sucre."*

Wartime food (that's World War II) has mostly faded from my mind. Miracles were wrought with minimum supplies, and almost everyone grew organic vegetables in the Victory Gardens. Women swapped recipes for eggless cakes, mock whipped cream and mock duck made from ground up whale. If you ate out, you might find rabbit masquerading as veal (or was it vice versa?).

Somehow I survived boarding-school food; even the one dietitian who served fried sandwiches (two slices of bread filled with jam, or a single slice of ham, cheese or canned corned beef, dipped in batter and deep-fried), more and more frequently until the day she was fired after serving fried sandwiches for breakfast, lunch and supper. During vacations, however, there was mother's roast pheasant, partridge casserole, and rich jugged hare (did I mention that we lived on a farm, and my father is a crack shot?), her sticky gingerbread and ragged-robin cookies On visits to my grandmother there was beautiful soup, steak and kidney pudding, shortbread, and tart-apple pie, spiced with lemon and speckled with currants.

I think it was at this time that I began to think seriously about food and cooking, including fantasizing what I would serve if I were suddenly made the school dietitian, or if I could turn grandmother's romantic house into a restaurant.

My mother pronounced that her two daughters might follow any career they chose (she herself has a degree in dairy science from Glasgow University), but at some point they had to learn to cook. Dismayed by the dull fare domestic-science schools offered, I fortunately ferreted out the Cordon Bleu school in London, and signed up for the longest (one year) course. Each morning we cooked a three-course meal, then sat down and ate it; the afternoons were devoted to English and American bread and cakes, French patisserie, and *haute cuisine* (The four-story climb to the kitchen prevented obesity). Right from the start, I was hooked on the magic of cooking and since then (to trim this autobiography), I have cooked in a school, taught at the Cordon Bleu, cooked in a Long Island restaurant and worked as a consultant. And for the last seven or eight years I have been food editor, first of *Look*, and more recently, of *Family Health* and *Redbook*.

I'm convinced that the most civilized and progressive approach to food is to learn to cook simple, basic foods well, and to organize meal-planning and cooking so that not too much time is spent on it. You'll be doing your children a favor if you involve them in food preparation, too. Good nutrition is so closely related to good health, that it's important to be selective about the food you buy and serve. Aim to get the most nutrition for your dollar. With today's agriculture, transportation and refrigeration, a wide variety of good fruits, vegetables, grains, fish, meat, poultry and dairy products are available year-round; it's largely a question of making the right choices.

What Are Healthy Foods?

Healthy foods are those whose inbred nutrients have been damaged or diluted as little as possible between farm and table. They are grown, processed, marketed and cooked in such a way that, when eaten, their nutrient content is as high as possible.

Take a potato for example. The nutrient content of a freshly dug potato is influenced by the seed's genes, the nutrient content of the soil, the climate, and the degree of maturity at harvest. Once out of the ground, a slow, but inevitable loss of nutrients begins, and from then on, the nutrient content of the potato you eat is further influenced by temperature conditions during its travels from farm to pot (in fresh, frozen or canned form), the length of storage time, and, of course, its final encounter with the cook.

It's true that a potato, as well as any other food, can be maltreated all along the line and still have some nutrients left when eaten. But a diet of foods that are not as nutritious as they could be, can lead to malnutrition. (It is also an incredible waste of nutrients.) When a man is described as "malnourished" it does not mean that he lacks *food*, but rather that his diet lacks *nutrients*. A malnourished person is in a less-than-good state of health, and, therefore, more prone to disease.

Today, although plenty of nutritious foods are available, many people are buying less nutritious ones. Think for instance, about the baked goods you buy. Crackers made entirely of whole-wheat or rye flour are much healthier than those made of white flour, even so-called enriched white flour. Why? To make white flour, the wheat germ and outer bran coating, which contain a very large proportion of the nutrient of the original grain, are sifted out. Even when white flour is enriched, only 4 of those lost nutrients are put back. So, of course, it makes sense to buy whole-wheat or rye crackers; they are available, and they are good to eat.

Vegetables that are washed quickly, peeled just before cooking, then steamed or cooked with very little water, will have more of their vitamins and minerals left when you eat them than if they are peeled hours ahead, left pitifully soaking, then overcooked in a huge pot of boiling water.

Peaches and tomatoes, picked and sold before they are fully ripened, the fate of so many today, have fewer vitamins than they would if allowed to ripen to their full genetic potential on the tree or vine.

Why Eat the Healthier Foods?

Why should we care about the food we eat? Why? Because although our genes determine to a large extent what we are, food does also, from the moment we are conceived. Food becomes you, even when you're an adult and have stopped growing—upward, at least. Everyday about 3 billion cells in the body die and must be replaced. All our cells, of which there are many different sizes and shapes, need a continuous supply of the 57 known nutrients to keep them operating in anything like top gear.

Health is a variable state that can range from terrible to terrific. While food is not the only factor in good health, it is one of the most important. Unfortunately, there are no miracle foods that guarantee instant health because there is no one perfect food. Building health and maintaining it is a continuing long-term project, not an instant one. We need to get into the life habit of buying and eating the more nutritious foods. This book aims to help in two areas: first in making the best choices in the marketplace, and, second, in nutrient conservation in the kitchen. Cooking with good nutrition in mind offers these advantages over common methods:

- shorter cooking times
- simpler cooking techniques
- superior flavors and textures in the food you serve

What can you do about what you eat? If you feel your own family fare could do with a major overhaul or even a slight improvement, don't, for heaven's sake, announce your decision at dinner. Don't immediately sweep all undesirable foods and candy out of the pantry. Instead, make the changes gradually. When that box of fried onion-flavored rings is empty, replace it with a healthier snack such as pumpkin seeds or whole rye crackers. When you need cereal, buy a brand that isn't sugar-coated or loaded with marshmallows—or you might try making your own. If you try baking bread, say you're doing it because you've always wanted to, not because you want to make a bread that's really good for the family. Try sneaking nutritious organ meats, like kidney and liver, onto the menu, perhaps mixed at first with other foods, familiar ones. Make the big changes gradually, and for a while at least, keep the secret to yourself.

Of course, food must give pleasure as well as provide nutrients. Sometimes it may be a matter of your palate growing up. Just as most of us were cautious the first time we sampled oysters or olives, so it may be the second time around before you realize that brown rice, for instance, has a much better flavor, as well as more nutrients, than white.

NUTRITION — A QUICK, HIGHLY SIMPLIFIED GUIDE

Nutrition is what we eat, and the effect on our bodies of the food we eat. A nutrient is anything that *nourishes:* proteins, carbohydrates, vitamins and minerals.

At the moment, about 57 chemical compounds are known or believed to be necessary to sustain human life. All 57 can be obtained from 7 general types of food, plus water. Each one of the 7 groups is an outstanding source of certain nutrients, a less valuable one for others. Yet this grouping is only a general guide because it cannot take into account the individual characteristics of certain foods. Liver, for instance, is a rich source of vitamin A, a vitamin more commonly found in dark green and yellow vegetables. Neither is the grouping very helpful when you are working with a product or recipe that mixes groups of food, such as spinach souffle made with spinach, eggs and milk. Perhaps the most important key to good nutrition is to eat a varied diet over the period of a week, a month or a year. One of the aims of this book is to help you enjoy foods you may not have tried before because you did not know how to prepare them. To help you in thinking about food and meal planning, here's a breakdown of the 7 groups:

MEAT, FISH, EGGS, POULTRY, DRIED BEANS AND PEAS, AND NUTS make up *the protein group.*

The proteins in food are made up from a total of 20 amino acids. All but 8 of these acids can be synthesized by the body from other foods. Meat, fish, eggs and poultry, contain all the 8 "essential" amino acids (that is, those which the body is not capable of making), and are known variously as "high-quality," "first-class," "animal" or "biologically-complete" proteins. Dried peas, beans and lentils, collectively known as *legumes,* do not contain all of the big 8 amino acids, but still are a low-fat source of valuable proteins. The body can use legume protein more effectively if it is accompanied by an "animal" protein in the form of meat, fish, milk or poultry. Legume proteins are also complemented by grain proteins, and it is interesting to note that many cultures that rely on legumes as their chief protein source have developed staple dishes that combine, say, rice and beans.

CITRUS FRUITS, TOMATOES, RAW CABBAGE, etc.—*the vitamin C group.*

The fruits and vegetables in this group, which also includes strawberries, green and red peppers, salad greens and cantaloupe, are our prime source of natural vitamin C.

They also supply generous quantities of other vitamins and minerals, including vitamin A, calcium and iron.

LEAFY, GREEN, AND YELLOW VEGETABLES—*the vitamin A group.*

Broccoli, asparagus, chard, kale, collard greens, turnip greens, green peas and string beans are in this group, as are carrots, winter squash, pumpkins, sweet potatoes, wax beans and yellow turnips (rutabagas). Besides the generous amount of vitamin A, many also provide iron, calcium, thiamin, riboflavin, niacin and vitamin C.

When planning meals, it's important to emphasize the fruits and vegetables in the A and C groups.

POTATOES AND OTHER VEGETABLES AND FRUITS

In this group are all the fruits and vegetables not in the two groups already covered, including beets, onions, celery, eggplant, corn, parsnips, cucumbers and white turnips. Fruits in this group include apples, grapes, peaches, pears, pineapple, figs, prunes, raisins, plums and bananas. Potatoes, if eaten baked or steamed, are an excellent source of vitamin C. This group provides generous amounts of vitamins and minerals, also many of the carbohydrates needed by the body. Fruits supply plenty of natural sugars.

MILK AND MILK PRODUCTS—the *calcium foods*

From fresh, dried or evaporated milk, yogurt, cheese or ice cream, we obtain the calcium necessary for development and maintenance of teeth and bones, and for well-functioning nerves. Milk products also supply good-quality protein, vitamin A (except for skim) and riboflavin. On the basis of the calcium they provide, 1 cup of milk (160 calories) is the approximate equivalent of 1 1/2 cups ice cream (382 calories), or 1 1/2 ounces Cheddar cheese (172 calories).

About 2/3 of the world's adult population do not tolerate milk well. If you are among them, you may be able to consume fermented milk products, such as cheese, homemade yogurt or buttermilk. If not, make sure you eat plenty of dark green vegetables to help supply calcium.

GRAINS AND CEREALS—*B vitamins and carbohydrates*

In this group are wheat, barley, rice, rye, oats, cornmeal and millet, made into flour, bread, crackers and cereal products. Use whole grains and whole-grain products whenever possible, as they contain a greater supply of vitamins and minerals than refined grains, and more of a better quality protein. When using refined grains, such as white flour, make sure it is unbleached and enriched.

BUTTER AND FORTIFIED MARGARINE

Sources of energy (as calories from fat) and vitamin A. Fortified margarine has enough vitamin A added to equal the amount normally found in butter.

HOW MUCH AND HOW OFTEN?

How many servings should you have from each group every day, and just what is a "serving?" Here's what the United States Department of Agriculture suggests:

Meat Group: two or more servings per person daily. Two to 3 ounces of cooked meat equals one serving; 2 eggs equal one serving.

Vitamin C group: one or more servings daily. One-half cup of vegetable or fruit, or juice, or a usual portion such as 1/2 grapefruit, equals one serving.

Vitamin A group: one serving every day or at least every other day. One-half cup makes one serving.

Other fruits and vegetables: two or more servings each day.

Milk groups: 1 cup is one serving. The USDA recommends 2 to 3 cups for children under 9, 3 or more cups for 9 to 12 years old, 4 or more cups for teenagers and 2 or more cups for adults.

Bread and cereal groups: four or more servings per person daily. One slice of bread or 1/2 cup cereal equal 1 serving.

The number of servings actually depends on the person's age, size and degree of activity. For example, a teenage boy and a man who has a physically very hard job, may require several average adult servings because of rapid growth or activity. A young child may need only about half an adult serving. The trick is to cover all the food groups, but to adjust total food intake to calorie needs.

WHAT IS A BALANCED DIET?

As no one food is perfect, and no single food group supplies a full quota of every known nutrient, the balanced diet is one that includes foods from each group each day, and preferably mixing protein, grains and vegetables or fruit at each meal.

DOES THE SAME DIET WORK FOR EVERYONE?

In our nutritional requirements, as well as in every other way, each of us is an individual. Nutrition is extremely complicated; a diet that makes one person healthy, slender and happy, may not work precisely that way for another. We have to work the details out for ourselves. As I see it, the most important maxim is to use a wide variety of foods, and not to serve them always in the same combination. Choose foods that give you plenty of nutrients to begin with, and cook them in such a way that the food will taste as delicious as possible, and retain as many nutrients as possible, feeding both body and soul.

WHAT YOU SHOULD NOT EAT—MAYBE

Cholesterol and saturated fats have been cast as the "bad guys" in explaining the current high rate of heart disease and other medical problems. The American Heart Association has even gone so far as to recommend that all Americans do something positive about their choice of foods in order to reduce the amount of cholesterol and saturated fats they eat. On the other side of the argument, certain experts have recently dismissed this position as based on unconclusive evidence.

Whatever the outcome of the debate, cholesterol is found only in products of animal origin such as meat, poultry, fish, eggs and milk. (Some margarines, made partly with animal fat, contain cholesterol.) The best approach seems to be to eat a wide variety of meats and fish; choose fish more often than shellfish, chicken or fish more often than beef; and don't go overboard on the organ meats, especially brains, as they tend to be high in cholesterol. Sometimes adult males are advised by their physicians to go easy on the number of eggs they eat.

With saturated fats the great problem probably lies in the large amount we eat without realizing it. Those described on food labels as "vegetable shortening" or "hydrogenated shortening" are saturated, or partially saturated, even if the oil from which they were made was unsaturated, because the process of hydrogenation (whipping hydrogen into oil to harden it) changes an unsaturated oil into a partially or completely saturated one.

Hydrogenated fats are found in almost all cookies, crackers, peanut butter, store cakes and pastries, mixes for cakes, frosting and pancakes; frozen and refrigerated milk shakes and shake bases, whipped toppings and imitation dairy products such as sour dressing (pseudo-sour cream), nondairy creamers and coffee whiteners.

Recently, research has suggested that refined sugar, besides contributing heavily to our gross national bulge, poor teeth and growing incidence of diabetes, may also play a role in heart disease. Dr. John Yudkin, University of London nutritionist, says that the evidence against sugar is even more conclusive than it is against cholesterol. Professor Jean Mayer of Harvard, suggests that it is not a question of fat *or* sugar, but of fat *and* sugar.

If you're using prepared foods such as cake and pancake mixes, where hydrogenated fat and sugar are the main ingredients, it may take quite an effort to make a change. But it will be worthwhile for plus reasons, too. For instance, regular pancake mix is made with white flour, shortening and sugar. If you make your own pancakes with yeast, honey, whole-grain flours and oil or butter, you *gain* very considerably in B, E and other vitamins, in calcium and even in protein quality and quantity.

A total switch to unsaturated fats in the diet does not seem advisable unless, of course, your doctor says otherwise. One study showed that persons on such a drastic diet did indeed lower their susceptibility to heart disease, but had a higher incidence of other major illnesses. Although we need some fat, a more Jack Sprat attitude could help reduce overall intake. Cut out fried snack foods such as potato chips, corn chips, and cheese squiggles. Cut down on battered- or breaded-and-fried foods. Choose the leaner cuts of meat; drink milk or eat yogurt more often than ice cream. Use yogurt in cooking more often than sour cream. A baked potato contains a worthwhile amount of vitamin C and other nutrients; it contains only about 1 percent fat. Fry that potato and you come out with something about 13 percent fat. Eat potato chips and the fat goes to about 40 percent; besides you end up not only with more calories but fewer nutrients, because vitamins and minerals are lost in the cutting, washing and frying of the potatoes. So, when you eat a wide variety of foods, make sure you eat them in a form supplying maximum nutrients, minimum added calories.

Don't be intimidated by the foregoing nutrition lecture, but just keep the ideas in the back of your mind. And don't be bludgeoned into feeling that you have to produce an elaborate meal every day. I submit that simplicity is the best policy, and few meals are better than one of roast or broiled chicken (providing the chicken has good flavor), fresh broccoli cooked only to a bright-green firmness, brown rice simmered in broth, and an excellent salad. Concentrate on the main course. Cook with care and love—for those you love.

ELIZABETH ALSTON LANSING
New York City

How to Live with This Cookbook

The symbol ‡ beside a recipe means I am trying to catch your eye to say "please try this." I always find myself in a quandary trying to decide which recipes to try first in a new cookbook. The symbol ‡ attempts to overcome my problem for you!

Always preheat the *oven* or *broiler*, unless a recipe specifies otherwise. Turn on 10 to 15 minutes before you expect to put the food in. Keep an oven thermometer in your oven, so you can check your oven's thermostat; if it's way off, a serviceman can fix it.

Use a *meat thermometer* for roasting meat; it saves much anxiety. Have at least one *kitchen timer* for the same reason. (You can check thermometers by putting them in boiling water; they should then register 212° F.)

When a recipe calls for *oil* without specifying a particular kind, use a basic oil such as corn or soybean. See the salad chapter and the shopping guide for salad oil suggestions.

To help you in marketing, the *approximate weight* of an ingredient is often given as well as the cup measure. Cauliflowers and cabbages, for instance, come in all sizes. *Garlic* does, too, and to overcome that problem garlic is specified in teaspoons and tablespoons. Peel one or two cloves of garlic, chop roughly, then measure.

When an ingredient such as a carrot is *diced,* cut it into fairly neat pieces, about 1/8-inch square. *Minced* onion, or anything, is cut into tiny pieces about 1/2 the size of a peppercorn. If you don't know how to chop an onion in the professional and quickest way, ask someone who does to show you how.

Onions are always peeled before chopping, potatoes and carrots not necessarily. Use a vegetable peeler for carrots and potatoes. Trim off the roots from scallions and the outer layer; use all the white part and about half of the green.

To *chop parsley,* hold the point of a French cook's knife down on the table with your left hand. Chop up and down (holding handle in right hand) and back and forth without lifting the point. Use a *stainless steel knife* for cutting acid fruits such as apples and pears. Have two or three *carbon steel knives,* French cook's shape, for most other work. Buy good knives that feel comfortable in your hand and keep them *sharp.*

Please buy a *steamer basket* or rack (same thing) if you don't have one. The best one has 3 adjustable legs (that I leave fully extended), a rigid rack and flexible sides. It is inexpensive. Lids of the pots you use it in must fit tightly to keep steam from escaping.

When liquid is *boiling,* it's 212° F., rolling and roiling. When the directions say *simmer,* bring the liquid just to the boil, then turn heat down until the surface of the liquid barely moves. *Poaching* is done at a lower temperature; only an occasional bubble should break the surface of the liquid.

*The Best of Natural Eating
Around the World*

1

The Healthy Breakfast

Most of us are incredibly narrow-minded about what tastes good for breakfast. It's usually eggs or cereal or toast and coffee, period. But in our house breakfast is one of the most enjoyable meals of the day. We may have chicken soup, broiled fish, cold chicken, oyster stew, clam chowder, sausage, cheese—almost anything you can think of that doesn't require too much preparation or can simply be heated through. Breakfast is a perfect time to serve leftover cold meat and fish. Not only does it solve the problem of what to have for breakfast, but you're saved the torture of worrying about "what can I do with this" for dinner. With good homemade bread and a slice of tomato, a couple of radishes or a sprig of watercress, leftovers can be delicious.

Another habit that needs breaking occasionally is the orange-juice-for-breakfast habit. A whole orange, just peeled, is more nutritious than juice of any kind. And how about having berries, an apple or a banana for breakfast and then, if you like, citrus fruit at dinnertime in a salad or dessert.

Here are some more ideas for breaking breakfast barriers.

Menu-Maker's Guide

To Start a Day Ahead:

‡ Black Beans with Cheese
Kedgeree
‡ Corn Meal and Whole-Wheat Pancakes
Chicken Noodle Breakfast Soup

Cereal (See also chapter on Grains):

Date Oat Cereal Blend
Sunflower Cereal
Almond Chia Cereal
‡ Crunchy Five-Grain Cereal

Pancakes:

‡ Cottage Cheese Pancakes
Swiss Pancakes
‡ Corn Meal Whole-Wheat Pancakes

To Make in Morning:

Split Peas
‡ Baked Ham and Eggs
‡ Chinese Clam Custard
Miso Soup

Breakfast from a Can:

Serve well-drained tuna, mackerel, salmon or sardines with whole-wheat bread, tomato wedges, celery sticks or watercress.

Look in fancy food stores for a very inexpensive cod roe pâté from Norway. Also smoked cods' livers from the same part of the world. Both are delicious.

Canned roast beef hash can be good too, though low on meat; use it when you have some leftovers of your own to add. Serve hot with a poached egg on top.

Breakfast from the Refrigerator

Serve cheeses, leftover meat or fish dishes with whole-wheat bread, tomato, watercress or other raw vegetables.

‡ BLACK BEANS WITH CHEESE

Soak and cook beans a day or two before you plan to use them.

1 1/2 cups dried black beans	*1 teaspoon salt*
3 cups water	*1 cup diced sharp cheddar cheese*

Soak beans in water 8 to 24 hours in refrigerator. Bring to a boil, add salt; cover and simmer until tender, 1 to 1 1/2 hours. Chill until needed. Shortly before serving, tip beans, plus any liquid, into a heavy iron skillet. Mash about 1/3 of them with a fork, while heating. When bubbling hot and thick, stir in cheese and turn off heat. Leave for 1 minute while cheese melts. Makes 3 cups. Serve as is, or with a half or whole hard-cooked egg per person. If you like, add chopped chili peppers, minced onion or garlic.

SPLIT PEAS

2 cups water	*1/2 teaspoon salt*
1 cup green or yellow split peas	

Bring water to a boil, add peas and salt. Simmer, covered for 30 to 40 minutes. Peas should be tender but not too mushy. Serve plain, with a poached egg on top, or with a piece of cheese, or include milk or yogurt in the meal. Makes 2 cups.

‡ CORN MEAL WHOLE-WHEAT PANCAKES

If you make the batter the morning you want to use it, instead of the night before, warm the milk slightly then make the batter as directed and let stand 20 minutes before cooking.

1 envelope yeast	*1 1/2 cups milk*
1/4 cup warm water	*1 cup stone-ground*
1/3 cup molasses,	*whole, yellow corn*
preferably not	*meal*
blackstrap	*1 cup whole-wheat*
1/4 teaspoon salt	*flour*
2 large eggs	

Prepare batter the night before: Mix yeast with warm water and molasses in a bowl. Let stand 2 to 3 minutes. Add salt, eggs, milk and corn meal. Stir until smooth, then stir in the whole-wheat flour. Cover bowl and refrigerate overnight. Next morning, stir the batter well—it will be bubbly. Heat a lightly oiled iron griddle or skillet. Drop batter, a quarter cupful at a time, into the skillet. When bubbles rise to the surface and break, turn the pancakes over and cook about 1 minute longer. Repeat with remaining batter. Serve with butter and honey, or applesauce and sour cream or yogurt. Makes 2 1/2 cups batter, about 10 pancakes.

‡ COTTAGE CHEESE PANCAKES

1 cup cottage cheese	*2 eggs*
1/2 teaspoon salt	*2 teaspoons honey*
1 tablespoon	
cornstarch	

Put all ingredients in electric blender and whir smooth. (This recipe does not require flour.) Heat an iron griddle or skillet and oil lightly. To do this, pour a few drops of oil into the skillet then wipe over the bottom with a rag or piece of paper towel. Drop the batter in tablespoonfuls onto the hot, oiled griddle. When brown underneath, turn pancakes over and brown on the second side. Repeat until all batter is made into pancakes. Recipe makes 1 1/4 cups batter, about 16 small pancakes. Serve with berries, sliced peaches, applesauce, or with honey and sour cream.

SWISS PANCAKES

4 tablespoons whole-wheat pastry flour	*1 1/2 teaspoons Dijon mustard*
1/2 cup sour cream	*1 cup (about 5 ounces) coarsely grated Gruyère or Switzerland Swiss cheese*
2 eggs	
Pinch ground nutmeg	
1/2 teaspoon salt	*Oil*

Using a small whisk, mix flour and sour cream in a bowl. Add eggs, nutmeg, salt and mustard; whisk smooth. Mix in the cheese. Heat an iron skillet or griddle, and oil very lightly. To do this, put a few drops of oil on the griddle or skillet, then wipe over the bottom with a small piece of paper towel or rag. Drop batter in full tablespoonfuls onto hot griddle. Cook about 2 minutes, then turn over and cook about 2 minutes longer. Pancakes should be brown on both sides. Repeat with remaining batter. Pancakes should be eaten right away. Recipe makes 1 1/2 cups batter, about 14 small pancakes. Serve with applesauce if you like, although they don't really need anything. They can also be served with a salad for supper.

DATE OAT CEREAL BLEND

6 pitted dates	*1/4 cup wheat germ, raw or toasted*
2 cups rolled oats	

Put dates in an electric blender, then add 1 cup of oats and the wheat germ. Whir until crumbly and broken up, about 1 minute. Mix with remaining rolled oats in a bowl. Serve with milk. Makes just over 2 cups.

SUNFLOWER CEREAL

Similar to above, just more exotic.

8 pitted dates	*2 tablespoons soy grits*
2 cups rolled oats	*1/4 cup millet flakes*
1/4 cup wheat germ	*(optional)*
2 tablespoons	
sunflower or	
pumpkin seeds	

Put dates in an electric blender, then add 1 cup of rolled oats, the wheat germ, seeds and soy grits. Whir until crumbly and broken up, about 1 minute. Pour into a bowl or storage container, then mix in millet flakes and remaining rolled oats. Makes 2 1/2 cups.

ALMOND CHIA CEREAL

Chia seeds are considered to be almost magical by some health food enthusiasts, but I've never felt any effect at all. These tiny seeds have little flavor and are awfully expensive, but if you want to try them, why not? One tablespoon could be added to the 2 previous recipes.

1/4 cup almonds or	*1/2 cup wheat germ,*
pecans	*raw or toasted*
2 teaspoons chia seeds	*1 tablespoon honey*
(optional)	*3/4 cup rolled oats*

Put all ingredients in electric blender in order given. Whir until well broken up. Stop machine once to stir mixture, if necessary. Makes 1 1/3 cups. Serve with milk and fruit.

‡ CRUNCHY FIVE-GRAIN CEREAL

*1 cup whole-wheat
 flour*
1 cup rye flour
*1 cup stone-ground
 whole yellow corn
 meal*
1 cup soy flour
1 tablespoon salt
1 1/2 cups rolled oats
*1/2 cup millet or millet
 flour; or hulled
 barley or barley
 flour*

*3 tablespoons unhulled
 sesame seeds*
1/4 cup honey
1/4 cup molasses
1/2 cup oil
1/2 cup water

Have ready one or two roasting pans or similar containers. Put the whole-wheat flour, rye flour, corn meal, soy flour and salt into a large mixing bowl. Whir oats in electric blender to break them up; add to bowl. Add millet or barley flour to bowl. (If using whole millet or barley instead, whir them first in blender to a gritty powder state.) Whir sesame seeds in blender to break up slightly. Add to bowl. Mix all together thoroughly. Now dump honey, molasses, oil and water on top. Use your hands to rub flours and liquids together, until mixture is an even crumbly mass looking something like dog kibble. Tip into the roasting pans and spread out to a depth of about 1/2 inch. Put in 250° F. oven and let bake for 1 to 1 1/2 hours. Shake or stir the cereal about three times during the hour. When done, cereal should be quite hard and dry. Let cool in pan before storing in an airtight container. Makes 7 cups crunchy, satisfying cereal. Serve with milk and fruit.

Chestnut Five-Grain Cereal: Add 3/4 cup chestnut flour to other flours, and 1/4 cup water to liquid called for in previous recipe.

KEDGEREE

3/4 to 1 pound smoked   3/4 teaspoon salt
    haddock fillet   1 tablespoon butter
  1 cup water
1/2 cup brown
    unpolished rice

Buy haddock that has not been dyed bright yellow. Bring water to boil in heavy pot, stir in rice and salt. Simmer covered until tender, about 45 minutes. No water should be left in pot. Meanwhile, put fish in a shallow pan or skillet; cover with cold water, bring very slowly to a simmer, then cook for 5 minutes. Drain, cool, then break into flakes with your fingers; discard any skin or bones. Mix cooked rice with fish and 1 tablespoon butter. Serve right away or chill overnight. To reheat, put kedgeree in top of double boiler, or set the bowl containing it in a pan of simmering water. Makes 3 to 3 1/2 cups. Kedgeree may be topped with chopped chives or with chopped hard-cooked egg (whole, yolk only or white only). Leftover rice and fish can be used for this dish in approximate proportions of 1 1/2 cups cooked rice, 1 1/2 cups cooked, flaked fish.

‡ BAKED HAM AND EGGS

   For each person: 1 slice Switzerland
1 slice boiled ham   Swiss cheese
1 egg

Put ham slice in bottom of an individual baking dish. Lay the slice of cheese (folded in half, if large) on top of the ham. Break the egg and drop on top of cheese. Bake for 10 to 12 minutes at 350° F., just until egg white is set. Serve right away. If you wish, several portions can be baked at once in a larger dish.

CHICKEN NOODLE BREAKFAST SOUP

*1 chicken, about
   2 1/2 pounds
6 cups water
2 teaspoons salt
1 cup sliced
   mushrooms
1 1/2 cups fresh or frozen
   green peas*

*About 4 ounces shirataki
(Oriental bean thread
noodles); or about 2 cups
cooked fine buckwheat or
other noodles*

Start the day before: split chicken down one side of back bone and open out flat. Put in a pan with water and salt. Bring to a boil, cover, and simmer 1 hour. Let cool in broth. Remove skin and bones from chicken (hands are best tools). There should be about 3 cups chicken meat, cut in bite-size pieces, and a good 4 cups broth. Refrigerate chicken and broth overnight. In morning, bring broth to boil. Add mushrooms and peas and simmer, uncovered, 5 minutes. Soak shirataki noodles, if used, in warm water for 5 minutes, then drain. Add chicken and noodles to broth and heat gently for about 5 minutes. Taste, add more salt if needed. Makes 8 cups soup. Stripped chicken bones can be simmered with water for an hour to make a weaker, but useful, "second" stock.

MISO SOUP

Miso is a fermented soybean paste, tofu is a bland soybean cheese; buy both at Oriental and health food stores. Some supermarkets sell canned tofu. Miso soup, with perhaps just a slice or two of mushroom floating in it, is the soup commonly offered as an appetizer in Chinese restaurants.

*2 cups water
1 to 2 tablespoons
   light or dark miso
   paste
1 cup thinly sliced
   carrots
   Large pinch hiziki
   seaweed (optional)*

*1 cup finely sliced
   cabbage
1 cup diced bean curd
   (tofu); or 1 cup
   diced raw or cooked
   fish*

Bring water and 1 tablespoon miso paste to a boil. Add sliced carrots. Simmer covered 3 minutes. Soak seaweed, if used, in a little warm water. Taste soup. Add remaining tablespoon of miso paste if you wish. Add cabbage and simmer covered 5 minutes. Add drained seaweed, bean curd or fish and heat through. Makes 3 cups thick soup. Onions, celery or other vegetables can be used instead of cabbage. Sliced mushrooms are a delicious addition.

‡ CHINESE STEAMED CLAM CUSTARD

If you prefer, custard mixture can be assembled in a bowl, then steamed in 4 one-cup dishes.

1 can (6 ounces) minced clams	*1/4* cup thinly sliced scallions
1 bottle (8 ounces) clam juice	*1 1/2* teaspoons soy sauce
Water	*1* teaspoon chopped parsley (optional)
4 large eggs	

Set a strainer over a 2-cup measuring cup and drain the clams into it. To clam liquid in measuring cup, add bottled clam juice, then water to make a total of 1 3/4 cups liquid. Pour into a pan and heat. In a 1-quart casserole dish, beat eggs with a small whisk or fork. Beat in hot broth, then stir in clams, scallions, soy sauce and parsley. Cover dish with foil or a small plate. Put about 1-inch of water in the bottom of a deep pan. Put a steamer basket in the pan and set the casserole dish on top of it. Bring water to a boil, cover pan, and let custard steam 20 to 25 minutes. Uncover dish and shake gently; custard is done if it shakes like gelatin and is no longer liquid in the center. Remove casserole dish carefully from pan. Serve custard hot or cold, spooning it onto plates; clams will be on bottom. Serves 4.

2

The Healthful Grains

Whole grains are rich in B vitamins, vitamin E, and minerals. Although health food stores usually carry a wide variety, and specialty and ethnic stores a smaller range, even the supermarket can be a source. Plain rolled oats for instance, are the whole grain. So are Maltex and Wheatena, two proprietary cereals.

For stone ground, whole, undegermed corn meal and natural brown barley, you will probably have to locate a health food store or mail order source. However most supermarkets carry brown rice. Even better and more delicious is a short-grain brown unpolished rice like that grown and packed by Chico-San.

The next best choice to brown rice is a *converted* rice such as Uncle Ben's. In the processing, many of the nutrients generally lost in polishing are forced into the grain. This is not true for other kinds of instant rice.

Cooking Grains

The simplest, plainest way to cook grains is in salted water in a heavy, tightly covered pot. The thick pot helps prevent the grains from sticking and scorching, and is easy to clean. Soak pan in water soon after removing the cooked grains.

To bring out their best flavors, grains should simmer gently. You can serve them plain, with a lump of butter stirred in, or add any number of seasonings while cooking or afterward.

The following table shows you what to expect from 1 cup of grain. Sometimes you can double the amounts exactly and sometimes not. Absorbency varies. If you are not following a recipe exactly, experiment cautiously. Usually you need proportionately less water as you increase the amount of grain. Cooking time however, remains the same.

Sometimes the age of the grain will affect the cooking time or the amount of water required, so times and quantities may vary slightly—even from one purchase of grain to another. Grains can be cooked in liquids other than water. Vegetable broth, meat broth, soup and juices can be used. If you use an acid liquid such as tomato juice you will have to allow more cooking time. The acidity tends to slow down the cooking, often quite a lot.

Grains that take approximately the same time to cook can be combined. Adjust the proportion of liquid if not the same for both.

Avoid sticky, gooey gelatinous cooked grains by subjecting them to high heat immediately. Either drizzle them into actively boiling liquid, or sizzle them in hot fat before adding boiling liquid. This abrupt confrontation will tend to seal the outer layer of starch and the grains will hold their shape better when cooked. Grains are "done" when they are tender, easy to chew and have a slightly translucent quality. *Whole* grains never get as soft as polished ones because of the bran, the tough outer layer of a grain (where many vitamins and minerals are stored) which is removed when a grain is polished or pearled.

To prevent finely ground grains like rice cream and corn meal from lumping, whisk them slowly into the hot liquid. This is easier than whisking the liquid into them.

1 cup cereal	Water	Makes	Cooking Time
Barley, hulled, not pearled. Any size.	3 cups	3 cups	60 minutes
Barley, natural brown	3 cups	3 cups	1 1/2 hours
Barley, flakes	2 cups	2 cups	10 minutes
Bulgur, cracked, parched wheat Coarse, medium or fine grind	2 cups	2 cups	15 to 30 minutes depending on grind
Buckwheat groats, also called Kasha	2 cups	2 cups	5 to 15 minutes
Corn meal, undegermed	2 cups	2 cups	20 minutes
Maltex	3 cups	3 cups	5 minutes
Millet, hulled	2 cups	4 cups	30 to 40 minutes
Oats			
H.O.	1 1/2 cups	1 1/8 cups	10 to 15 minutes
Steel cut	3 cups	3 cups	20 to 30 minutes
Rolled, such as Quaker	2 cups	1 1/3 cups	5 to 10 minutes
Rice, unpolished brown, not white	2 cups	3 cups	35 to 45 minutes
Rice cream, brown, made from brown rice	5 cups	5 cups	20 minutes
Rye, whole kernels*	2 cups	3 cups	1 1/2 hours
Wheat Flakes (look like rolled oats)	2 cups	2 cups	5 to 10 minutes
Wheat, whole kernels*	2 cups	3 cups	1 1/2 hours
Wheatena	4 cups	4 cups	5 to 10 minutes

*sometimes called ryeberries and wheatberries

No recipes are given for whole-wheat or rye grains because they take hours to cook and, in our frank opinion, taste simply dreadful. *Cracked* wheat or rye tastes delicious and is "whole grain." Wheat grains are delicious when sprouted and made into bread (see recipe for Sprouted Wheat Bread, p. 00).

Ideas for ways to vary basic grains. Add any of the following just before serving: nuts browned in butter, stir-fried onions, sautéed mushrooms, shredded raw carrot, shredded cheese (Parmesan or sharp Cheddar), toasted sesame seeds, hulled sunflower seeds, currants, grated lemon or orange peel, braised celery, sour cream, bits of meat or seafood, poppy seeds and butter, yogurt, wheat germ, minced fresh herbs, crumbled nori seaweed, soaked hiziki seaweed, orange segments, chopped tomato, crisp crumbled bacon, bits of vegetable.

Menu-Maker's Guide

Several dishes can serve as either an accompaniment or a main dish, and therefore appear in more than one category.

Main Dishes:

Clam Rice and Millet
Chicken Millet
‡ Polenta with Meat Sauce
‡ Corn Meal Tomato Bake
Corn Meal Cakes
Down South Raisin Rye
Cracked Rye Canadian
Kasha
Kidney with Kasha and Bulgur
Mushroom Barley
Oatmeal and Chipped Beef
Scallion Cheese Maltex

Grains For Breakfast:

Carrot Rice Cream
Polenta
Corn Meal Cakes
Cracked Rye Canadian
Kasha
Oatmeal and Chipped Beef
Scallion Cheese Maltex
Apple Wheatena

Snacks:

‡ Sizzled Rice
Corn Meal Cakes

Grain Dishes To Accompany Meat Or Vegetable Dishes:

‡ Sizzled Rice
  Spicy Rice
  Celery Tomato Rice
‡ Garlic Rosemary Rice
  Carrot Rice Cream
  Clam Rice and Millet
  Polenta
  Down South Raisin Rye
  Cracked Rye Canadian
  Kasha
  Kidney with Kasha and Bulgur
‡ Mint Pea Bulgur
  Mushroom Barley
  Barley Bones
  Scallion Cheese Maltex
  Apple Wheatena

‡ SIZZLED RICE

This is the rice-lovers' popcorn. Best picked up in fingers. Crisp and crackling, it's good with salad or soup. Take a bagful to the movies. Can be made with leftover rice.

> 2 **cups water**
> 1 1/2 **teaspoons salt**
> 1 **cup (6 ounces)**
> **brown rice, long or**
> **short grain**

Bring water to a boil in a small heavy pot. Stir in rice and salt. Reboil, then lower heat and simmer covered 35 to 45 minutes until tender, but still slightly chewy. No water should be left in the pan. Spread cooked rice out on a cookie sheet or roasting pan. Bake in a 400° F. oven for 30 minutes. Stir well every 10 minutes. When rice is a rich gold color and tends to clump, it is ready. Serve warm. Makes 1 1/2 cups.

SPICY RICE

Serve as an accompaniment to meat or vegetable dishes.

2 tablespoons olive oil
2 teaspoons chopped
 garlic
1 1/2 teaspoons salt
1/4 teaspoon ground
 cumin
1/32 teaspoon cayenne
 pepper; or
 2 tablespoons
 minced fresh chili
 pepper
1 cup minced onion

1/2 cup finely chopped
 parsley, preferably
 Italian
1 jar (4 ounces)
 pimiento, drained
 and finely chopped
3 1/2 cups meat broth; or
 3 1/2 cups water
 with 2 bouillon
 cubes
2 cups (12 ounces)
 brown rice

Heat oil in a heavy 1 1/2-to 2-quart pot. Add garlic, salt, cumin, cayenne or chili pepper, onion, parsley and pimiento. Stir-fry over medium high heat for 5 minutes. Stir in broth or water and bouillon cubes. Bring to a boil. Stir in rice. Reboil, then lower heat and simmer covered 35 to 45 minutes. Makes 6 cups.

CELERY TOMATO RICE

Serve as accompaniment to a fairly plain meat or salad as it has a very savory flavor.

3 cups tomato juice
1/2 teaspoon salt
4 peppercorns
3 whole cloves
 2-inch bay leaf

1 cup chopped celery
 tops and/or stalks
1 cup (6 ounces)
 brown rice

Bring tomato juice to boil in a heavy 1 1/2- to 2-quart pot. Stir in salt, peppercorns, cloves, bay leaf, celery and rice. Reboil, then lower heat and simmer covered for 1 hour and 15 to 20 minutes, until rice is tender but still slightly chewy. Fish out the bay leaf; peppercorns and cloves will probably have disappeared. Makes 4 cups.

‡ GARLIC ROSEMARY RICE

Good served with plain broiled chicken.

1 teaspoon chopped garlic	*1 teaspoon lemon juice*
1 teaspoon salt	*1 teaspoon dried*
1 tablespoon oil	*rosemary, or a*
1 tablespoon butter	*2-inch sprig of fresh*
1 1/2 cups (9 ounces) brown rice	*3 cups boiling water; or vegetable*
1/4 teaspoon finely grated lemon rind	*or chicken broth*

On a board with the blade of a knife crush garlic with salt to a smooth paste. Heat oil and butter in a heavy 1 1/2- to 2-quart pot; add garlic and salt and stir-fry 1 minute. Add rice and stir-fry 3 minutes. Add lemon rind, juice, rosemary and broth to pot. Simmer covered 35 to 45 minutes until just tender. Makes 4 1/2 cups.

CARROT RICE CREAM

This is rather sweet like yams. It's good for breakfast as well as a side dish at dinner. Brown rice "cream" is brown rice ground to a very fine powder.

2/3 cup (3 3/4 ounces) brown rice cream	*or 3 cups fresh carrot juice*
2 cans (12 ounces each) carrot juice;	*2 tablespoons butter*

Put rice cream into a heavy 1 1/2- to 2-quart pot or top of double boiler. Beat carrot juice, a little at a time, into the rice cream. Use a wire whisk if necessary to keep mixture smooth.

When all the juice is beaten in, add the butter. Bring mixture to boil over low heat or boiling water (if using double boiler). Stir constantly. Turn heat very low and simmer covered 20 minutes. Makes 3 1/3 cups.

CLAM RICE AND MILLET

Tastes quite strong, like stuffed clams without the clams. Serve alone like a pasta course or with a salad.

2 tablespoons olive oil	1/2 cup (3 ounces)
1/4 teaspoon salt	brown rice
Black pepper	1/2 cup (2 ounces)
1/2 cup thinly sliced	hulled millet
leek	1/4 cup finely chopped
2 bottles (8 ounces	parsley, preferably
each) clam juice; or	Italian
2 cups fresh	

Heat oil in a heavy 1- to 2-quart pot. Add salt, a little black pepper, leek and clam juice and bring to boil. Stir in rice and millet. Reboil, then lower heat and simmer covered 35 to 45 minutes until tender. Stir in parsley. Makes 3 cups.

Main Dish Fish Pilaf: Prepare previous recipe, then stir in 1 to 2 cups (1/2 to 1 pound) cubed raw cod, or other white fish, 5 minutes before serving. Or stir in a dozen or more shucked clams.

CHICKEN MILLET

The amount of chicken can be increased if you wish.

1 tablespoon oil	1 teaspoon salt
1 pound (about 6)	Black pepper
chicken thighs or	2 cups water
other parts	1 cup (4 ounces)
1 cup (about 5	hulled millet
ounces) chopped	
green pepper	

Heat oil in a heavy 2- to 3-quart pot. Add chicken parts and brown 2 to 3 minutes each side. Add to pan the green pepper, salt, a good grating of black pepper and water. Bring to a boil. Stir in millet. Reboil, then lower heat and simmer covered 30 to 40 minutes, until millet is tender but not mushy. Makes 4 cups millet, plus chicken.

POLENTA

Polenta can be made with half milk, half water to increase the protein. In some Italian homes, enormous quantities of thick, crusty polenta are spread directly onto a freshly scrubbed, wooden kitchen table. Generous quantities of a rich meat sauce are ladled over the polenta, then everyone eats directly from the table.

> **4 cups water**
> **2 teaspoons salt**
> **2 cups (10 ounces)**
> **stone ground whole**
> **yellow corn meal**

Bring water to a boil in a heavy 1 1/2- to 2-quart pot, or in a heavy iron skillet. Add salt to water then slowly whisk in the corn meal. For a soft polenta, cook corn meal very slowly for 20 minutes tightly covered. For a crusty polenta, cook uncovered over low heat 20 to 30 minutes until a tasty outer edge and bottom form and the corn meal pulls away from the sides of the pan. Makes 4 cups.

‡ *Polenta with Meat Sauce:* Serve wedges of crusty polenta with a meat sauce or tomato sauce and Parmesan cheese. A meat sauce containing hot Italian sausage is especially good.

Polenta for Breakfast: Chill cooked polenta. In morning, cut in slices and fry in butter.

Polenta with Cheese: Spread cooked polenta in a baking dish. Top with plenty grated Cheddar cheese and put under broiler just until cheese is melted. Serve with salad for a meatless main dish. Delicious for breakfast.

Polenta with Meat: With roast or broiled meat, serve either plain polenta, cut in wedges or sliced-and-fried polenta.

‡ CORN MEAL TOMATO BAKE

Serve as a main dish accompanied by a large crunchy salad. If you use canned tomatoes bake at 350° F. until firm, about 1 hour, instead of as directed.

1 1/2 cups water; or
    1 cup water, 1/2
    cup milk
  1 cup (5 ounces) stone
    ground whole yellow
    corn meal
  2 cups chopped fresh
    tomato
	2 eggs
	  1 teaspoon honey
	1 1/4 teaspoons salt
	    Black pepper
	  1 tablespoon butter

Bring water to boil in a heavy 1 1/2- to 2-quart pot. Slowly pour corn meal into boiling water while whisking constantly. Remove pan from heat; stir in tomato. Beat in eggs, honey, salt and a good grating of black pepper. Grease a 1-quart baking dish with butter. Pour in corn meal mixture. Bake in a 375° F. oven for 45 minutes until firm. Makes 4 cups.

CORN MEAL CAKES

Serve corn meal cakes with syrup for breakfast, with your carrot juice at cocktail time or with applesauce for supper.

1 cup boiling water
1/4 teaspoon salt
  1 cup (5 ounces) stone
    ground whole yellow
    corn meal
	1/2 cup cold milk
	    Butter

Bring water and salt to boil in a small heavy pot. Slowly pour in corn meal, whisking constantly. Then whisk in milk. Remove pot from heat. Melt butter in a skillet to generously cover the bottom. Drop corn meal mixture into the butter in tablespoonfuls. Fry corn meal cakes 2 to 3 minutes each side over medium heat until golden. Drain on paper towel and serve hot. Makes 20 corn meal cakes.

DOWN SOUTH RAISIN RYE

Serve this as a main dish. Ham hocks are short on meat, so if you wish, stir in 1 cup or more diced, cooked ham during last 5 minutes of cooking.

Serve also as an accompaniment to ham or chicken, without extra diced ham.

1/2 pound smoked ham hocks (about 2 good-sized pieces)	**1/3 cup raisins** **4 cups water** **2 cups cracked rye**

Put ham hocks, raisins and water in a heavy 2-quart pot and bring to a boil. Sprinkle in cracked rye. When boiling, lower heat and simmer covered 45 minutes until tender. Taste, and add salt if necessary. Makes 4 cups rye.

CRACKED RYE CANADIAN

Serve as a main dish, accompanied by vegetables, or serve with meat. Good for breakfast, too.

1/2 pound (1 cup) Canadian bacon, cut into cubes **1 tablespoon caraway seeds**	**4 cups water** **2 cups cracked rye**

Stir-fry bacon cubes in a heavy 1 1/2-quart pot for 2 to 3 minutes until lightly browned. Add caraway seeds and water; bring to a boil. Stir in cracked rye. When boiling, lower heat and simmer, covered, 45 minutes until tender. Taste and add salt if necessary. Makes 5 cups.

KASHA

Serve for breakfast, dinner or any time.

2 **tablespoons oil or**	*1* **egg, if you like**
other fat	2 **cups boiling water,**
3/4 **teaspoon salt**	**broth, or**
1/2 **cup finely chopped**	**liquid from cooking**
onion (optional)	**vegetables**
1 **cup (5 ounces)**	2 **more eggs, if for**
buckwheat groats	**main course**
(kasha)	

Heat oil in a heavy 1 1/2-quart pot. Add salt and onion (if using) and stir-fry 2 minutes. Stir in buckwheat groats and fry 1 minute until very hot. Break egg and drop on top of kasha; stir in quickly. Stir in water or broth. Simmer covered 1 to 15 minutes until tender. Watch carefully and do not let it go to mush. If using 2 additional eggs stir them in and let kasha sit covered for 3 minutes. Makes 4 cups.

KIDNEY WITH KASHA AND BULGUR

Serve as a main dish with a salad. Or serve with a plain meat such as turkey where you need a rich-tasting accompaniment. Two cups of either kasha or bulgur may be used instead of 1 cup of each.

1 **beef kidney (12 to**	**Black pepper**
15 **ounces)**	*1* **cup (5 ounces)**
3 **tablespoons oil or**	**buckwheat groats**
other fat	**(kasha)**
1/2 **cup minced onion**	*1* **cup (5 ounces)**
1/2 **teaspoon allspice**	**bulgur (parched,**
1/4 **teaspoon ground**	**cracked wheat)**
cinnamon	2 **cups boiling water**
1 1/2 **teaspoons salt**	

With knife or scissors cut kidney away from core of white fat; mince finely to make about 1 cup. Heat 2 tablespoons of the oil in a heavy 2-quart pot. Add onion, allspice, cinnamon, salt and a good grating of black pepper. Stir-fry 2 minutes. Add kidney to pan, stir-fry over low heat 2 minutes. Lift kidney and onion out of pan onto a plate and keep on hand. Add remaining tablespoon of oil to pan. Add kasha and bulgur and stir-fry until each piece is hot and coated with oil. Stir in boiling water. Simmer covered 10 minutes. Stir in kidney and onion. Simmer covered 5 minutes until water is absorbed and kidney just cooked. Makes 6 cups.

‡ MINT PEA BULGUR

Serve as an accompaniment to meats or vegetables. This dish also can be made with Maltex or Wheatena.

2 cups water	*1 cup (5 ounces)*
1 1/2 teaspoons salt	*bulgur (cracked*
Black pepper	*parched wheat), any*
1 tablespoon crumbled	*grind*
dried mint leaves or	*2 cups fresh peas or 1*
2 tablespoons	*package (10 ounces)*
minced fresh mint	*frozen green peas*
leaves	*1/2 cup sour cream*

Bring water, salt, a little black pepper, and mint to boil in a heavy 1 1/2-quart pot. Stir in bulgur, reboil, then lower heat and simmer covered 10 minutes. Stir in peas; simmer covered 5 to 10 minutes until all water is absorbed and both cereal and peas are tender. Remove pot from heat. Stir in sour cream. Makes 4 cups.

BARLEY BONES

Serve barley as an accompaniment to meat dishes.

1 to 2 pounds marrow	*1-inch bay leaf*
bones, preferably	*1 onion*
with soft center	*2 cloves*
4 cups water or	*1 1/3 cups (8 ounces)*
vegetable broth	*natural brown or*
1 1/2 teaspoons salt	*hulled barley*
4 peppercorns	

Marrow bones are large beef soup bones with soft marrow centers; ask the butcher to help identify. Put bones in a roasting pan and brown them in a 400° F. oven for 30 minutes. Then bring water to boil in a heavy 2-quart pot. Add bones, salt, peppercorns, bay leaf, onion with the 2 cloves stuck in it and the barley. Stir to moisten barley. Reboil, then lower heat and simmer, covered, for 1 to 1 1/2 hours. Lift out bones and scoop out soft centers; stir gently into barley. Discard bones, and cloves if not disintegrated. Makes 4 cups barley.

MUSHROOM BARLEY

Serve as an accompaniment or main dish. If you like, stir in a little chopped almonds, pignolia nuts or wheat germ just before serving.

If you wish, omit the bacon and use 2 to 3 tablespoons oil or butter instead of the bacon fat.

> 2 *strips thickly sliced*
> *bacon or*
> 4 *strips thinly sliced*
> *bacon*
> 1/4 *teaspoon sage*
> 1 *teaspoon salt*
> 3 *peppercorns*
> 1 *pound mushrooms*
> *(4 to 5 cups sliced);*
>
> *or* 1 *can (8 ounces)*
> *mushroom pieces,*
> *drained*
> 3 *cups water*
> 1 *cup (6 ounces)*
> *natural brown or*
> *hulled barley*

Fry bacon crisp in a heavy 1 1/2-quart pot. Remove and drain. Stir sage, salt, peppercorns, and mushrooms into bacon fat. Stir-fry over medium heat for 5 minutes. Add water and bring to a boil. Stir in barley. Reboil, then lower heat and simmer, covered, 1 to 1 1/2 hours. Top with crumbled bacon. Makes 4 cups.

OATMEAL AND CHIPPED BEEF

This tasty dish makes a good breakfast, lunch or dinner.

2 tablespoons oil or
  other fat
1 cup chopped onions
1 teaspoon marjoram
1/2 teaspoon ground
  mace
1/2 teaspoon paprika
1/2 teaspoon dry
  mustard

Black pepper
1 jar (2 1/2 ounces)
  dried chipped beef,
  torn into bits (1/2
  cup)
4 cups water
1 1/3 cups (6 1/4 ounces)
  steel-cut oatmeal

Warm oil in a heavy 1 1/2-quart pot. Add onions, marjoram, mace, paprika, mustard and a grating or two of pepper. Stir-fry over medium heat for 2 minutes. Stir in chipped beef and stir-fry 1 minute longer. Add water and bring to a boil. Stir in oatmeal, lower heat and simmer, uncovered, for 10 minutes. Stir, cover, and simmer 20 minutes more. Makes 4 cups.

SCALLION CHEESE MALTEX

Looks weird but tastes just fine. Serve as a main dish, or as an accompaniment to meat and fish. Good and nourishing for breakfast.

3 cups water
1 teaspoon salt
1 cup thinly sliced
  scallions

Black pepper
1 cup Maltex
1 cup creamed cottage
  cheese

Bring water, salt, scallions and a good grating of black pepper to a boil in a heavy 1 1/2-quart pot. Stir in Maltex, reboil, then lower heat and simmer, uncovered, 5 minutes. Turn off heat, cover pan and let stand 5 minutes. Stir in cottage cheese. Makes 4 cups.

APPLE WHEATENA

Serve this sweet and spicy cereal for breakfast or as an accompaniment to meat or fowl.

3 tablespoons butter	1/4 teaspoon ground
1 teaspoon salt	cumin
1/2 teaspoon ground	4 cups apple juice
coriander	1 cup Wheatena

Melt butter in a heavy 1 1/2-quart pot. Add salt, coriander and cumin; stir-fry 30 seconds. Add apple juice and bring to a boil. Whisk in Wheatena, then lower heat and simmer, uncovered, stirring occasionally for 10 minutes until thick. Turn off heat, cover, and leave 5 minutes before serving. Makes 4 cups.

3

The Comfort of Soup

To me, soup is one of the loveliest and most comforting of foods. Somehow it always seems to go right into the bloodstream! Making soup for someone is always an act of love for me. To cook fresh vegetables as a soup feels like a primitive, basic, human way of preparing food.

The influential soup makers in my life have all been Scots—especially my paternal grandmother who still makes soup almost every day for lunch. Today, freshly made soup can play a very important part in the healthy way of eating. It is an appetizing way to include a wide variety of foods in the diet. By keeping cooking times to a minimum you retain as many vitamins and minerals as possible in the vegetables and meat used. Soup is good for breakfast, lunch or supper.

When you take a close look at soup recipes they come down to 2 main types: smooth creamy soups where the main ingredients are cooked and puréed, and thick, chunky soups where the vegetables and perhaps meat, too, are visible and recognizable.

Puréed soups can be made with almost any vegetable—carrots, leeks, potatoes, mushrooms, spinach, and so on. A glance at the recipes given here for parsley and Jerusalem artichoke soups, reveals that they are basically the same. You can use this knowledge, and the proportions given, to make soups from other vegetables.

In chunky soups, when meat is used, it is simmered ahead in water until tender. The water, flavored by the meat, becomes broth and contains some of the nutrients from the meat. Vegetables in this kind of soup are cooked for only a very short time at the end. Follow the suggested quantities closely the first time around so you see how the various flavor combinations "balance out." When you make your own variations, keep in mind that carrots and onions add a slightly sweet taste, too much celery can overshadow other vegetables, and turnip, if a lot is used, can dominate everything. Note, too, that some vegetables take longer to cook than others.

People who are picky about eating vegetables rarely feel that way about vegetable soups. If your family's menus are short on vegetables, a good soup to start a meal can help improve the situation.

To make soups as nutritious as possible keep in mind:

1. Cut up vegetables just before you add them to the soup. Don't let cut vegetables stand exposed to light and air longer than you have to. If you do cut them up a little ahead of time, cover them tightly and refrigerate.

2. The electric blender is an enormous help in making puréed soups. It not only saves you work, it makes more nutritious soups. Without a blender, vegetables need longer cooking because they must go through a strainer or food mill. And apart from the physical effort required, there is usually more waste with a strainer or food mill.

3. Chopped parsley added at the last minute to soup gives it flavor, color, and extra vitamins—parsley is an excellent source of vitamin A. To save time, chop a whole bunch at once (first removing the tough stems), then freeze what you don't immediately need.

4. To add protein to an all-vegetable soup try these ideas: cut Cheddar, Muenster, Mozzarella or Monterey cheese into tiny 1/8-inch cubes. Put about 2 tablespoons in the bottom of each bowl just before ladling in the boiling-hot soup. The cheese will melt and become creamy. Or, make egg-drop soup. Beat 1 or 2 eggs in a bowl for every 2 persons you will serve. Just before

serving, pour the eggs into the simmering soup in a stream, then remove from the heat immediately.

5. Among canned soups, the split pea, bean and lentil varieties offer good protein value. Include some small amount of first-class protein in the meal or snack, such as a glass of milk, a chicken sandwich, or a piece of cheese so the bean protein can be used more efficiently by the body.

6. The word "stock" calls forth visions of chefs, giant pots and long hours. Actually stock can be made surprisingly easily. However it is hard to *always* have it when you need it. So try various brands of canned chicken broth and look for bouillon cubes without monosodium glutamate. Canned consommé is too highly flavored to make a successful substitute for broth.

Menu-Maker's Guide

Soups speedily made for lunch, an after-school snack, or to quickly assauge hunger pangs:

The-Children-Will-Be-Home-for-Lunch-in-Five-Minutes Soup
Hidden Potential Soup
I'm Hungry-What-Can-I-Eat? Soup

The next 5 recipes make 10 to 12 cups each and are suitable for main dishes, or at least to play an important part in a menu. Besides, if you're going to cook lamb breast or the beef heart, you might as well end up with a large amount of soup for the effort. If you have a small family, remember that all these soups reheat well:

‡ Heart and Barley Soup (start the day before)
Chicken, Dried Pea and Vegetable Soup (start the day before)
Scotch Broth (start the day before)
Summer Vegetable Soup
‡ Russian Vegetable Borscht

Purée soups, quick to make, suitable for a first course at supper or for lunch:

Jerusalem Artichoke Soup
‡ Parsley Soup
‡ Broccoli Buttermilk Soup

Lentil and pea soups. Use for a light main course, or as a first course when a menu needs more protein:

Yellow Split Pea Soup
‡ Chick Pea Soup with Garlic, Mint and Parsley
Red Lentil Soup

Cold and Salad soups.

‡ Chilled Parsley Tomato Soup
‡ Broccoli Buttermilk Soup
Plum Pineapple Soup

Thick vegetable soups for lunch or dinner.

‡ Russian Vegetable Borscht
Summer Vegetable Soup
Sweet-Sour Pepper-Tomato Soup

THE-CHILDREN-WILL-BE-HOME-FOR-LUNCH-IN-FIVE-MINUTES SOUP

Also comforting as an after-school snack on a cold, rainy day.

2 cups tomato juice	1/2 cup coarsely
1/2 cup coarsely	chopped carrot
chopped celery	1/2 teaspoon salt
1/2 cup coarsely	1 cup milk
chopped green	
pepper	

Put 1 cup of tomato juice in the electric blender. Add the celery, green pepper and carrot. Whir to break up vegetables, but don't let mixture get too smooth. Pour into a saucepan; add salt and remaining cup of tomato juice. Bring just to a simmer; let cook about 3 minutes. Add milk and heat through. Makes 3 cups.

HIDDEN POTENTIAL SOUP

Tastes good, and the highly nutritious kidney is undetectable.

1 lamb kidney	*3 sprigs parsley*
2 cups chicken broth	
1/2 cup coarsely	
chopped green or	
red pepper	

Remove thin white outside skin from kidney, if butcher has not already done so. Slice kidney in half and snip or cut out the white fat. Rinse kidney briefly, then put in electric blender with remaining ingredients. Whir smooth. Pour mixture into a saucepan, bring to a simmer and cook 1 minute. Serve. Makes 2 cups.

I'M-HUNGRY-WHAT-CAN-I-EAT? SOUP

1 cup beef or chicken	*1/4 cup milk*
broth	*1 teaspoon chopped*
2 tablespoons soy	*parsley*
granules	

Mix broth and soy granules in a small saucepan; bring to a simmer. Cook 5 minutes. Add milk and parsley. Heat through. Makes 1 cup. A grated carrot can be added to the broth for last 3 minutes of cooking.

‡ HEART AND BARLEY SOUP

Heart is a delicious dark meat with beefy flavor and texture. Like liver, it is especially nutritious.

2 pounds beef soup bones, the kind with scraps of meat on them	2 cups diced carrots (about 1/2 pound)
	1 cup chopped onion (about 1/4 pound)
8 cups cold water	1 cup celery, sliced
2 1/2 teaspoons salt	1/8-inch thick
2/3 cup natural brown barley	(about 2 stalks), or, 1 cup diced celeriac
1 1/2 pounds beef or calf heart	1/2 cup chopped fresh parsley

The day before you wish to serve the soup, put beef bones, cold water and salt in a large, heavy 5-to-6-quart pot. Bring slowly to a simmer then cook, covered, for 1 hour. Add barley; simmer, covered, 1 hour longer. Add heart and simmer, covered, 1 hour longer. Cool, then chill overnight. About 30 minutes before serving, remove and discard fat from top of broth. Ladle about 2 cups of the broth into another pan; bring to a simmer, add carrots, onion and celery and simmer, covered, 10 to 15 minutes. Meanwhile, remove and save meat from bones. Trim any fat, skin or tiny tubes from heart, and dice heart meat. (You should have about 3 cups meat total). Bring meat slowly to a simmer in the barley broth. When vegetables are tender, add to the heart and barley and heat together 2 to 3 minutes. Taste; add parsley and more salt if you wish. Makes 10 cups thick soup. This soup reheats well and freezes well.

CHICKEN, DRIED PEA, AND VEGETABLE SOUP

My mother ate a soup similar to this one almost every Sunday during her childhood in Scotland. It was her father's task after church (her uncle was the minister) to chop the parsley picked from the garden. He always chopped it "as fine as mices' feet."

1 fowl, about 4
  pounds, thawed if
  frozen
Water
Salt
6 to 8 parsley stems
1 cup whole yellow or
  green dried peas
1 cup diced carrots
  (about 1/4 pound)
1 cup sliced onion
  (about 1/4 pound)

1 cup sliced leeks
  (about 3 ounces), if
  available
1 cup diced celery
  (about 2 stalks)
1/2 cup diced yellow
  turnip, or
  hamburg-parsley
  root
1/2 cup chopped fresh
  parsley

One or two days before you plan to serve soup, rinse bird, neck, gizzard and heart, and put into a heavy 5- to 6-quart pot that is deep rather than wide. Add 7 cups water, 4 teaspoons salt and the parsley stems. Bring to a simmer, cover and cook slowly for 1 1/2 hours. Meanwhile, put dried peas in a small pot with 2 1/2 cups water; simmer, covered, for 1 hour. Drain and rinse peas, add to fowl and let simmer together 1 hour longer. Cool, then chill. About 30 minutes before you wish to serve the soup, scoop fat off top of broth and discard. Ladle about 2 cups of the broth into another pot and bring to a simmer. Add cut-up vegetables and simmer, covered, just until tender, 10 to 15 minutes. Meanwhile, with your hands, remove fowl meat from bones; discard skin and bones. Break meat into bite-size chunks (you'll have 4 to 5 cups), put back in pan with peas and broth and heat through. Add cooked vegetables and let all simmer together 2 to 3 minutes. Taste; add more salt if you wish. Add parsley and serve. Makes about 12 cups.

SCOTCH BROTH

*4 pounds breast of
   lamb*
12 cups water
2 tablespoons salt
About 12 parsley stems
*1/2 cup natural brown
   barley*
*1 cup diced carrot
   (about 1/4 pound)*
*3/4 cup diced celery
   (about 1 1/2 stalks)*
*1 cup sliced leek
   (about 3 ounces), if
   available*

*3/4 cup diced yellow
   turnip (about 3
   ounces)*
*1 cup sliced onion
   (about 1/4 pound)*
*1 1/2 cups fresh or frozen
   green peas (part of
   a 10-ounce package)*
1/8 teaspoon marjoram
*1/4 cup chopped fresh
   parsley*

One or two days before you plan to serve the soup, put the lamb breast in a large heavy pot with the water, salt and parsley stems. Bring to a simmer, then cook covered for 1/2 hour; add barley and continue simmering (with lid on) for another 1 1/2 hours. Cool, then chill. About 30 minutes before serving, lift off and discard fat from top of lamb broth. With your fingers, separate fat and bones from lamb meat.* Discard fat and bones. Ladle about 3 cups of the lamb broth into another pot; bring to a boil, add vegetables, except peas, and simmer, covered, until just tender, about 10 minutes. Add peas and marjoram, simmer 2 minutes longer. Meanwhile, put lamb meat back in pot with barley and remaining broth. Heat slowly without boiling. Add the cooked vegetables and heat all together for about 5 minutes. Taste; add more salt or some pepper if you wish. Add chopped parsley and serve. Makes about 12 cups.

*Removing the lamb meat from the bones is a miserable chore, but you get about 4 cups of very inexpensive meat for the effort. If it's more convenient, you can do it ahead, keep meat and broth chilled until time to heat through.

SUMMER VEGETABLE SOUP

8 cups water
1 pound green beans
1 1/2 pounds zucchini
and/or summer
squash
1 1/2 tablespoons salt
1 cup small elbow
macaroni or
broken-up spaghetti

1 can (15 ounces)
navy beans or
cannellini, packed
in water, drained*
Pistou Sauce
(below)
Freshly grated
imported Parmesan
cheese

Bring water to boil in a 5- to 6-quart pot, preferably one you can serve from. Meanwhile, trim green beans and cut into approximately 1-inch lengths. Trim ends from squash, and cut into slices 1/2-inch thick. (You will have about 6 cups squash and 4 cups green beans). When water boils, add salt, macaroni, squash and green beans. Reboil quickly, then lower heat and simmer, covered, for 8 minutes. Add navy beans and simmer 8 minutes longer. Serve at once with Pistou Sauce and Parmesan cheese on the side. Makes 12 cups.

Pistou Sauce: Mix 1 cup peeled and chopped fresh tomatoes, or 1 can (8 ounces) tomatoes, with 1/2 teaspoon dried basil or 1 tablespoon chopped fresh basil. Salt to taste.

---

*Or, simmer 3/4 cup dried navy beans in 2 cups water for 2 hours with lid on. No need to soak.

‡ RUSSIAN VEGETABLE BORSCHT

8 cups broth
1 cup carrots, in
    1/8-inch slices
    (about 1/4 pound)
3 cups diced raw beets
    (about one 1 1/4
    pound bunch)
1/2 cup celery, sliced
    1/8-inch thick
    (about 1 stalk)
1/2 cup diced parsnip
    (about 2 ounces)
1 1/2 cups sliced onion
    (about 6 ounces)
1-inch bay leaf

5 cups coarsely
    shredded white
    cabbage (about 1
    pound)
3 tablespoons tomato
    paste
1 teaspoon honey
1 teaspoon salt
2 tablespoons
    unbleached white or
    whole-wheat pastry
    flour
1/3 cup sour cream
3 tablespoons chopped
    fresh parsley

Use homemade meat or vegetable broth, or use 8 cups water
and 8 chicken bouillon cubes. Bring broth to boil in a heavy
6-quart pot, preferably one you can serve from. When broth is
boiling, add all at once, the carrots, beets, celery, parsnip, onion
and bay leaf. Reboil quickly, then lower heat and simmer, covered, for 15 minutes. Add cabbage and simmer, covered, 18
minutes longer. Stir in tomato paste, honey and salt. Mix flour
with sour cream in a bowl and mix in a little hot soup, then add
all to the soup. Stir and simmer for 1 minute. Add parsley and
serve. Makes 12 cups.

JERUSALEM ARTICHOKE SOUP

1 pound Jerusalem
    artichokes*
2 cups water

2 teaspoons salt
4 cups milk

Scrub artichokes but do not peel. Rinse well and then cut into
fairly large chunks. Put in a pot (not aluminum) with water and
salt. Bring to a simmer, then cook, covered, until artichokes are

*A knobbly, delicious root vegetable available in some health food stores and farm markets.

tender, 10 to 15 minutes. Add 1/2 cup of the milk and pour mixture into an electric blender. Whir smooth, return to pot, add remaining milk and heat through. Makes 6 cups.

‡ PARSLEY SOUP

1 cup coarsely
   chopped parsley*
1 1/2 cups water or mild
   broth
1 tablespoon butter

1 tablespoon
   unbleached white or
   whole-wheat pastry
   flour
1 cup milk
1 teaspoon salt

Bring parsley and water to boil in 1 1/2-to-2-quart pot. Lower heat and simmer, covered, 7 minutes. Pour mixture into electric blender and whir briefly. Add remaining ingredients and blend again. Return to pan. Simmer 5 minutes. Serve hot. Makes 2 1/4 cups.

‡ BROCCOLI BUTTERMILK SOUP

2 cups thinly sliced
   broccoli, flowers and
   stems
1/2 cup diced green
   pepper
1/4 cup chopped onion

1 1/4 cups water
1/2 cup buttermilk
1 cup light cream
1/8 teaspoon curry
   powder
1 teaspoon salt

Trim any very tough, woody stems from broccoli, then cut into thin slices from top to bottom. Put in a 2-to 3-quart pot with green pepper, onion and water. Bring to a simmer, then cover and cook for about 10 minutes. Pour into an electric blender and whir smooth. Pour back into pot; add buttermilk, cream, curry powder and salt. Heat through without boiling. Makes 3 cups. Delicious hot or chilled.

---

*Before chopping parsley, discard tough bottom stems, but leave tender top ones. Press coarsely chopped parsley tightly down in cup to measure.

YELLOW SPLIT PEA SOUP

A pure-tasting, delicious soup. Serve it with cheese or ham, whole-grain bread and a salad.

1 cup yellow split peas	*1 teaspoon salt*
3 cups water	

Put all ingredients into a pan. Bring to a simmer; stir, cover and cook 30 minutes. Makes 2 1/2 cups.

‡ CHICK PEA SOUP WITH GARLIC, MINT AND PARSLEY

A fantastic soup. It can be made with 3 1/2 cups canned chick peas (a 1-pound can yields about 2 cups). Or you can use navy or other white beans. When using canned cooked chick peas or beans, omit the soaking and 1 1/2 to 2 hours cooking, and start by heating beans with their liquid in the chicken broth.

1 1/2 cups dried chick peas	*leaves from about 1 small sprig fresh mint*
3 1/2 cups water	
Salt	
4 cups chicken broth	*1/4 cup parsley sprigs, packed down to measure*
1/4 cup olive oil	
1/2 plus 1/8 teaspoon dried crushed mint leaves; or	*3 teaspoons chopped garlic*

Soak chick peas in water in refrigerator for 8 to 24 hours. Then put in a pot, bring to a simmer, add 3/4 teaspoon salt, and simmer, covered, for 1 1/2 to 2 hours. (This can be done ahead). Add chicken broth; heat. Put into an electric blender: the olive oil, mint leaves, parsley, garlic and 1/2 teaspoon salt. Add about 1 1/2 cups of the chick peas, and 1 cup of the liquid; blend until smooth. Pour back into pot and heat just to a simmer; do not boil. Makes 6 cups.

PLUM PINEAPPLE SOUP

1/2 pound purple plums
1 cup canned
pineapple juice

Remove pits and put plums into electric blender with the pineapple juice. Whir smooth. Serve right away or chill for 30 minutes. Soup is best eaten within 2 hours after making. Makes 2 cups.

RED LENTIL SOUP

The blending isn't essential, but it does bring all the flavors together.

3/4 cup red lentils
2 cups water
1 teaspoon salt
1/2 cup diced carrot
1/4 cup diced celery

Pinch thyme or
oregano
1/2 cup milk
1/2 cup nonfat dry milk

Heat lentils, water and salt in a pot. Simmer, covered, 20 minutes. Add carrot, celery and thyme; simmer, covered, 10 minutes longer. Pour into electric blender and whir smooth. Mix milk with nonfat dry milk in the cooking pot. Stir in puréed lentils and heat all together. Makes 4 cups soup. Serve with croutons, if you wish.

‡ CHILLED PARSLEY TOMATO SOUP

4 cups chilled canned
or fresh* tomato
juice
1/2 cup celery
1/2 cup parsley sprigs,
packed down tight
to measure

1/4 cup lemon juice
4 teaspoons honey

*If you use fresh tomato juice, add salt to taste.

Put all ingredients in electric blender and whir until smooth. Pour into a bowl, then cover and chill 20 minutes in freezer. Makes 4 cups.

SWEET-SOUR TOMATO-PEPPER SOUP

1 tablespoon oil
1/2 cup finely chopped onion
1 cup finely chopped sweet red or green peppers
2 cups water
1/2 cup thinly sliced okra (optional)

1 pound ripe tomatoes (plum tomatoes are best)
Salt
Cider vinegar
Cayenne pepper or Tabasco sauce (optional)
Pepper

Warm oil in a heavy 2- to 3-quart pot. Stir in onion and peppers. Cook, covered, over medium heat until translucent but not brown, about 2 minutes. Add water and bring to a simmer. Cook covered 2 minutes. Add okra, if used, and simmer 3 minutes longer. Meanwhile, add tomatoes to a pan of boiling water. Count slowly to 10, then pour off the boiling water and fill pan with cold water to stop cooking. Peel off skins, then chop tomatoes coarsely. Add to soup and heat through. While soup is heating, taste and season it: start by adding 1 teaspoon salt, 1 tablespoon vinegar, dash cayenne pepper or Tabasco sauce and a little black pepper. Taste, and season more highly if you wish. When tomatoes are hot, soup is ready. Makes 4 cups.

4

What's for Dinner?

Main Dishes

Most main dishes begin with meat, fish or poultry. These ingredients gobble up chunks of money, so it's doubly important to choose them wisely and to make the most of them when we use them. As so often is the case, good cooking methods go hand in hand with good flavor and good nutrition. Chicken cooked too long and at too high a temperature is less tender, flavorful and nutritious than chicken cooked at a moderate temperature just until done. Fish boiled in an ocean of water is tasteless and tough; it's also less nutritious than fish poached directly in a sauce because some of the nutrients, along with most of the flavor, go down the drain with the water.

Perhaps because the financial outlay can be high, we're often afraid to try new main dishes and are apt to get into a rut. One solution is to enlarge your repertoire of basics: Have you ever tried neck of lamb, lamb kidney or beef heart, or taken the plunge with squid?

As you probably already make many healthy main dishes, the emphasis in this book is laid on using some of the less common meats and on good cooking methods. Keep in mind:

1. Don't overcook meat. In meatball recipes for instance, the meat is often cooked for a long time. It's better to simmer the sauce first, then poach the meatballs in it for just 10 to 15 minutes. Ground meat has had all it's connective tissues broken up by the grinder, so longer cooking isn't going to make much difference to tenderness.

2. Fish and meat cooked in liquids, should poach, not boil. Once contents of the pot are simmering, the heat should be reduced so that just an occasional bubble breaks the surface. Maintaining this low heat can be tricky.

3. When a recipe calls for cooking meat in a lot of liquid, such as brisket of beef, remember the liquid will contain some nutrients from the meat. Either serve it in cups along with the meat, or use it later as a soup stock. You may like to try steaming brisket in a steamer basket over water, rather than in it.

4. To avoid the danger of salmonellosis and trichinosis, chicken, pork and pork products must always be completely cooked. Don't *overcook* them to a tough, dry state, but just until there's no trace of pinkness in the middle or near a bone. Sometimes the meat of very young chickens is dark red near a bone; this is not dangerous and should not be confused with pink, translucent-looking undercooked meat. When cooking roasts, try to use a meat thermometer. It saves lots of anxiety and helps ensure the meat is neither undercooked nor overcooked.

5. Meats such as lamb shanks or veal breast can be poached one day, and chilled until the next when all fat can easily be removed. This makes the finished dish more attractive to eat, as well as lower in calories.

6. Always reheat food carefully without letting it boil hard. At the most, it should simmer for a few seconds.

7. Ingredients vary tremendously, from chicken to chicken and carrot to carrot, so always taste sauced and multi-ingredient dishes before you serve them, and adjust the seasoning if you think it's not quite on target.

Menu-Maker's Guide

Thirty Minutes or less, from start to finish:

Garlic Butter Kidneys
‡ Liver with Sweet Peppers and Onions

Liver Spaghetti Sauce
‡ No-Bone Cod, Dill Sauce
‡ Haddock au Gratin
‡ Scrod in Rich Mushroom Sauce
‡ Italian Seafood Stew
‡ Cod Chowder
San Juan Baked Fish
Shrimp with Bean Sprouts and Other Things
Ardie Rodale's Sukiyaki
Basil Sauce for Pasta (Pesto)

More than 30 Minutes:

‡ Kidney, Sausage and Mushroom Casserole (45 minutes)
‡ Heart with Cholo Sauce (1 hour 15 minutes; or cook heart ahead)
Sweetbreads with Braised Prunes (1 hour 15 minutes)
Shrimp with Almonds in Coconut Milk (1 hour any time for coconut, then 30 minutes to finish)
Soy Ginger Baked Chicken (1 1/2 hours, mostly baking in oven)
‡ Chicken with Greens (40 minutes)
Basque Lamb Stew (1 1/2 hours)
Almond Spiced Lamb (45 minutes)
Bulgur-Mushroom Stuffed Flank Steak (30 minutes preparation, 1 1/2 hours cooking)
Organ-ized Meat Loaf (20 minutes to prepare, bake 2 hours)

Marinated Dishes:

Piquant Broiled Chicken (marinate 2 hours, cook 30 minutes)
Indian Roast Chicken (marinate 1 hour, cook 1 1/2 hours)
‡ Lamb with Yogurt, Cardamom and Coriander (marinate 1 hour cook 35 minutes)

The Insides Story

Apart from the familiar muscle meat, a carcass has the makings of many fine dishes in the organ meats. These meats are particularly rich in iron and B vitamins. Liver is also especially rich in vitamin A. Liver, kidney, brains and sweetbreads need only very short cooking; heart and tongue take longer.

KIDNEY

All kidneys are good to eat, but lamb and veal are the most delicate in flavor. Lamb kidneys are usually very inexpensive; veal kidneys may be costly in a luxury-apartment neighborhood, quite reasonable a few blocks away. Veal and beef kidneys have a large center core of hard white fat; to prepare them, cut the meat off the fat in bite-size chunks. Lamb and pork kidneys are the traditional kidney-shape. To prepare, cut them through the middle to make two kidney-shaped halves, then use scissors to snip out the white core. Cook kidneys for a very short time; if overcooked they get chalky and begin to smell rather strong.

‡ KIDNEY, SAUSAGE AND MUSHROOM CASSEROLE

Sauce may be prepared ahead then reheated to a simmer before adding kidneys. If your family is wary, cut kidneys into 1/8-inch thick slices for maximum invisibility.

1 pound white onions, peeled (about 16 if they're large, 24 if small; small onions are preferable)	1/2 cup chicken or beef broth
	2 tablespoons dry Sherry wine
	2 teaspoons tomato paste
1/2 pound little link pork sausages	1 2-inch bay leaf
6 lamb kidneys	Salt
1/4 pound mushrooms	Pepper
1 tablespoon whole-wheat pastry flour or unbleached white flour	2 tablespoons chopped parsley

Put onions in a steamer basket over 1/2 inch of simmering water in a pan. Cover and steam until tender—10 to 20 minutes. Meanwhile, fry sausages until brown in a 10-inch lidded skillet.

Rinse kidneys, cut in half, snip out fat and white core. Wipe mushrooms with damp cloth, (no need to peel) and trim a sliver off each stem. Leave small mushrooms whole; halve or quarter larger ones. Remove sausages from skillet and pour off almost all the fat. Add mushrooms and cooked onions to skillet, shake slowly over medium heat until lightly browned, about 2 minutes. Stir flour into the fat in the skillet, let brown about 1 minute. Stir in broth, sherry wine, tomato paste and bay leaf. Simmer, covered, 10 minutes. Stir sauce; taste and add salt and pepper if needed. Stir in kidneys and sausages; cook, covered, 5 minutes longer. Sprinkle with parsley. Serves 6. Good with broiled tomato halves and spinach or potato pancakes.

GARLIC BUTTER KIDNEYS

Four veal kidneys may be used instead of lamb kidneys. If so, halve them lengthwise, then cut into 1/2-inch cubes discarding the core of white fat.

10 lamb kidneys	1 tablespoon oil
1 tablespoon plus 1 teaspoon chopped garlic	1/3 cup water or broth
	1 tablespoon butter
	1/4 cup chopped parsley
1 teaspoon salt	

Rinse kidneys quickly in cold water and pat dry. Cut in half and snip out the white core. Cut each kidney into 1/4-inch thick slices. (This can be done ahead, and kidneys refrigerated). With the blade of a knife, crush garlic with salt on a board to a smooth paste. Heat oil in a 10-inch skillet. Add kidneys, and cook over high heat 3 to 4 minutes. Stir once or twice. Add water or broth to skillet; stir to incorporate any brown bits off the bottom. When bubbling, turn down heat. Stir in butter, garlic and parsley; heat without boiling. Taste, add more salt if you wish. Serve at once to 4.

HEART

Heart has a rich, beefy flavor. It can be cut in small chunks and added to beef stew, or ground and mixed with ground beef for spaghetti sauce, meatballs, meat loaf, etc.; mix 1 pound of ground beef with 1/4 pound of ground heart. Veal (calf) heart is tender enough to fry or broil: Cut the trimmed heart into 1/4-inch thick slices, or into French-fry shapes. Pan fry or broil as is, or first marinate in a herb marinade, or brush with a barbecue sauce.

‡ HEART WITH CHOLO SAUCE

*2 pounds beef or calf
    heart (cut in slices
    1-inch thick)
2 tablespoons oil
1 1/2 cups chopped onions
1 cup currants or
    raisins
1 teaspoon minced
    garlic*

*1/4 cup chopped canned
    green chili peppers
    (part of a 4-ounce
    can)
1/2 cup sliced stuffed
    green olives
3 cups (1 1/2 pounds)
    canned tomatoes*

Put heart in a steamer basket over 1 inch of simmering water in a pan. Cover pan tightly. Let simmer over medium heat until meat is tender: 30 to 40 minutes for calf heart, about 1 hour for beef. (This can be done a day or two ahead). Heat oil in a heavy 3-quart pot. Stir in onion and let brown slowly, 7 to 10 minutes. Add raisins (or currants) and garlic; stir until raisins are shiny and plump, about 1 minute. Add chili peppers, olives and tomatoes to the pot; break up tomatoes with a spoon. Let sauce simmer, covered, for 30 minutes. Cut off any fat and straggly pieces from cooked heart. Cut heart into 1/2-inch cubes, add to sauce and heat through over low flame for about 5 minutes. Makes about 5 cups, serves 4 to 6. Serve with plain rice or millet and follow with a cool, refreshing salad.

SWEETBREADS

This delicate organ tastes something like chicken. Sweetbreads are sold by the "pair" with a pair weighing about 1 to 1 1/4 pounds. Like veal kidneys, the price can vary from store to store by as much as a dollar per pound. Many recipes call for a preliminary parboiling but this is not necessary. First pull off any excess connective tissue, then cut sweetbreads into 1-inch slices or pull into bite-size chunks. Sweetbreads can then be simply fried in butter for about 6 minutes over medium heat, or brushed with butter and broiled.

SWEETBREADS WITH BRAISED PRUNES

8 *to 10 small white*	*1 cup good broth*
onions	*1/2-inch bay leaf*
1/2 tablespoon butter	*1 pair (1 to 1 1/4*
8 *soft prunes*	*pounds) calf*
1/2 tablespoon	*sweetbreads, thawed*
unbleached white	*if frozen*
flour	*1/4 cup chopped parsley*
1/4 cup dry red wine	

Put unpeeled onions in a steamer basket in a pan over 1/2 inch of boiling water. Cover pan tightly and let onions steam until almost tender, about 8 minutes for tiny onions, 20 for larger. Melt the butter in a heavy pot or lidded skillet. Add peeled onions and sauté over medium heat until lightly browned, 4 to 5 minutes. Add prunes and stir over heat 1 to 2 minutes. Stir flour into butter in pan; let brown slightly, about 2 minutes. Add wine, broth and bay leaf; stir until sauce is simmering. Cover and let cook slowly for 30 minutes to develop a good rich flavor. Trim sweetbreads of any raggedy bits and excess connective tissue; pull into bite-size chunks. Add to sauce and cook, uncovered, 5 to 10 minutes longer. Add parsley and serve. (If sauce is very runny, remove cooked sweetbreads to serving dish, turn up heat and let sauce boil fast for a minute or two until it is shiny and coats the onions. Spoon over sweetbreads.) Serves 4.

LIVER

Liver, when purchased, should be dark-colored and bloody. If pale and dry-looking it may have been washed off a couple of times in the market. Calves liver, though expensive, is mild-flavored and may therefore be worth buying for novice liver eaters. Buy it thinly sliced (1/4-inch thick); a good butcher will remove any visible tubes. Liver is good fried and served with crisp bacon. Pour off fat from skillet after cooking bacon. Brown liver quickly on one side; turn over and cook a minute or so longer. Liver is best when it's still slightly pink on the inside. It is good with baked or steamed potatoes and buttered broccoli. If the family likes barbecue dishes, dip cubes of beef or calves liver in a barbecue sauce, then quickly broil or pan-fry. Or spear the raw cubes on skewers and broil to make liver kabobs.

‡ LIVER WITH SWEET PEPPERS AND ONIONS

3/4 to 1 pound calves or lamb liver, sliced 1/4- to 1/2-inch thick	*2 teaspoons unbleached white flour*
1 pound yellow onions	*Black pepper*
1 pound sweet red or green peppers	*1 1/2 teaspoons salt*
3 tablespoons oil	*1 tablespoon plus 1 teaspoon cider, or rice, vinegar*

Liver and vegetables can be cut up ahead of time, covered and refrigerated until needed. Cut liver slices across to make strips about the size of a French fry. Slice onions 1/8-inch thick, then separate rings with fingers. Halve peppers, remove seeds and stem and cut into strips 1/8-inch wide. About 10 minutes before serving, heat 1 tablespoon of oil in a heavy 10-inch skillet or large pot. Add liver, sprinkle with flour and a grating of black pepper. Cook over fairly high heat 2 to 3 minutes; turn once. Cook until just pink in the middle then tip out onto a platter and keep warm. Add remaining oil to skillet, stir in onion rings, pepper strips and salt. With a spoon in each hand, stir-fry vegetables for 1 minute. Cover skillet tightly, cook over medium heat until vegetables are crisp-tender, about 2 minutes. (No water should be necessary.) Put liver back into skillet and add vinegar. With two spoons, toss contents of the skillet over fairly high heat for about 1 minute to heat through and blend flavors. Serve at once to 4 to 6.

LIVER SPAGHETTI SAUCE

Sauce can be made ahead, then reheated carefully.

1 tablespoon oil
3/4 cup finely chopped onion
1 tablespoon unbleached white or whole-wheat pastry flour
1 cup strong chicken or beef broth
1/4 teaspoon chopped garlic

1/4 teaspoon salt
1 teaspoon tomato paste
2 teaspoons Sherry or Marsala wine, optional (more is not better here)
3 parsley stems
Tiny pinch thyme
1/4 pound calves liver
Black pepper

Warm oil in a small, heavy 1- to 1 1/2-quart pot. Stir in onion; cook, covered, over medium heat until translucent and soft, 3 to 4 minutes. Uncover, let onion brown slowly, 5 to 7 minutes; stir occasionally. Stir in flour, then broth. With the flat of a knife crush garlic and salt to a smooth paste on a board. Add to pot. Add all remaining ingredients, except liver and black pepper. Let sauce simmer, uncovered, for 10 minutes until flavor is strengthened and volume reduced. Meanwhile, chop liver finely; remove and discard any "tubes." Stir into sauce and cook *below* simmering point for 5 minutes, just until liver is firm. Season sauce with black pepper and serve. Makes 1 1/4 cups, enough for 2.

Fish

High in good-quality protein and low in saturated fat, fish can appear often on the healthy menu. When you question fish-haters, it usually turns out they either had a bad experience with bones as a child or they can't stand the smell of fish cooking. Recipes using fish fillets are a good way to introduce children to fish and to avoid unhappy experiences. And if your kitchen reeks, you are probably overcooking (fish needs very little cooking), or using too high a temperature.

Simple broiling is an excellent way to cook fish, especially oily fish such as salmon, mackerel, fresh tuna and shad.

‡ NO-BONE COD, DILL SAUCE

Use any white, unoily fish such as haddock, cod, scrod, sole or flounder. I sometimes make shrimp this way for breakfast. It's a fine recipe for boneless frozen fish; let thaw just until you can cut it into 1/2-inch cubes. Don't let the sauce boil once the fish is added; if you do, the sauce will thin considerably and the fish acquire that "fishy" flavor. But don't get scared—the recipe couldn't be easier.

> 3 tablespoons butter or oil
> 3 tablespoons unbleached white or whole-wheat pastry flour
> 2 cups milk, whole or skim
> 1 teaspoon dried dill

> weed, or about 3 tablespoons fresh dill cut finely with scissors
> 1 teaspoon salt
> 1 to 1 1/2 pounds skinless, boneless cod

Melt butter in a heavy 2- to 3-quart pot. Remove pot from heat. With a small wire whisk or wooden spoon, stir flour into butter. When smooth, pour in milk all at once. Put pot back on heat and bring sauce to boil, whisking, or stirring, constantly. Sauce will thicken and should be quite free of lumps. When sauce boils, turn down heat, add dill and salt and let simmer for 2 minutes. Cut fish into 1-inch cubes. Mix very gently into sauce with a spoon. Cover and let poach over very low heat for 5 to 6 minutes. Sauce should be below simmering point, not even bubbling. To check if fish is cooked, lift out a piece and break open. Center should be white, not translucent. Makes about 3 cups. (Sometimes I use 1/4 cup each butter and flour in this recipe, although that's a bit generous for weight-watchers.)

‡ *Haddock au Gratin:* Omit dill from previous recipe. Just before adding fish to sauce, stir in 1/2 teaspoon Dijon mustard. When

fish is almost done, gently stir in 1 cup grated sharp Cheddar cheese. Turn off heat, let stand for 1 minute. Pour into baking dish. Mix 2 tablespoons more grated cheese with 2 tablespoons breadcrumbs; sprinkle over fish. Broil 1 to 2 minutes until cheese browns. Makes about 3 cups. Use any white fish, scallops or crabmeat.

‡ **Scrod in Rich Mushroom Sauce:** Make as for cod in dill sauce, but omit dill. Add fish to sauce and cook 5 minutes. Gently stir in 4 ounces mushrooms, finely chopped (about 1 1/2 cups). Cook 1 minute more. Makes about 3 1/2 cups. Use any white fish or scallops.

‡ ITALIAN SEAFOOD STEW

In spite of lengthy directions for preparing the squid—an inexpensive friend tasting very much like lobster—this dish is quick to make. If you wish, make the vegetable and tomato base ahead; prepare the fish, and keep it chilled. Just before serving, reheat the tomato base and add fish as directed.

Suggested combination of fish—alterable at whim:

1/4 pound scallops	*1 can (1 pound)*
1/4 pound medium-sized shrimp	*peeled plum tomatoes*
1/4 pound white fish, such as cod or scrod	*1/2 cup water*
1/2 pound squid	*1 teaspoon chopped garlic*
1 tablespoon oil	*1/8 teaspoon salt*
1/2 cup finely chopped green pepper	*1 pound cherrystone clams, opened but*
1/4 cup finely chopped onion	*left on the half-shell*
1/4 cup finely chopped celery	

Prepare the fish: Halve or quarter the scallops if large. Peel and devein the shrimp. Cut the fish into strips approximately 1/2-inch square and 2-inches long.

Now, face up to the squid; pull or cut off tentacles just in front of eyes. Discard hard beak from center of tentacles. Now, with your fingers, clean out the white sac and remove the "backbone," a beautiful piece of equipment that looks like clear plastic. Quickly wash tentacles and empty sac, rubbing off any black skin. Leave tentacles whole; cut sac into 1/4-inch circles.

To make stew: Warm oil in a heavy 3-to 6-quart pot. Stir in green pepper, onion and celery; cook for 2 minutes. Add tomatoes and water; break up tomatoes with a spoon, then simmer, covered, 5 minutes. On a board with the flat of a knife, crush garlic with salt to a smooth paste. Add to pot with squid. Cook, covered, 3 minutes. Stir in shrimp, scallops and clams on the half-shell. Cook, covered, 3 minutes longer. Stir in fish strips and heat stew just enough to cook fish, about 1 minute. When stew begins to bubble again, it is ready. Makes 6 cups, serves 3 to 4 as a main dish. Serve with garlic bread, or with rice.

‡ COD CHOWDER

2 *tablespoons butter*	1/4 *teaspoon thyme*
1 *cup chopped onion*	1 *teaspoon salt*
1 *cup diced raw*	1 *pound fillet of any*
potatoes (peeled or	*white fish,*
not)	*such as cod or*
1 *cup milk*	*haddock*
1 *cup light cream*	

In a heavy 2- to 3-quart pot, melt butter and stir in onions. Cook, covered, over medium heat till onions are soft but not brown, about 3 minutes. Add potatoes, milk, cream, thyme and salt. Simmer, covered, 20 minutes. Potatoes should be just tender. Cut fish into 1/2-inch squares. Add to pot. Simmer 2 minutes only. Makes 4 cups. Serves 2 as a main dish soup.

SAN JUAN BAKED FISH

6 *whole fish, such as snapper or striped bass, cleaned but with heads left on, weighing about 12 to 16 ounces each*	1/2 *cup water*
	1/2 *cup olive oil*
	3/4 *cup sliced onions*
	2 *two-inch bay leaves*
	12 *small green pitted olives*
1 *teaspoon chopped garlic*	1 *tablespoon each of capers, and liquid from jar*
1 *teaspoon salt*	
1/4 *cup fresh lime juice*	*Black pepper*

Heads are left on fish for decoration, but if you can't face them, have them beheaded, by all means. Rinse fish in cold water and pat dry with a paper or cloth towel. Lay in a single layer in a lightly oiled baking dish. With the blade of a knife on a board, crush the garlic to a smooth paste with 1/2 teaspoon of the salt. Put in a bowl with remaining 1/2 teaspoon salt, lime juice, water, olive oil, sliced onions, bay leaves, olives, capers, caper liquid and black pepper; mix all together and spoon over fish. Bake for 10 minutes at 550° F.; turn heat down to 425° F. and bake 7 to 10 minutes longer. Be careful not to overcook. Serves 6 or more.

SHRIMP WITH ALMONDS IN COCONUT MILK

A very delicate, delicious dish. Minus fish or shellfish, the sauce can be served over rice for a no-meat main dish. To remove coconut from shell, pierce the two soft "eyes" with a skewer; drain out the liquid. Bake coconut for 1 hour at 250° F. If shell has not cracked open, a sharp rap should do the trick. Meat will have shrunk from shell. Meat will keep at least 1 week refrigerated, longer frozen. (See recipe for Toasted Coconut, page 000.)

1 tablespoon oil	1/8 teaspoon ground cumin
1 cup minced onions	
1 tablespoon finely chopped garlic	1 1/2 teaspoons salt
1/2 cup shelled almonds	1 1/2 to 2 pounds medium-sized shrimp, peeled and deveined, or a combination of shrimp and boneless cod
1 1/2 cups cut-up fresh coconut meat	
1 1/2 cups boiling water	
1 teaspoon ground coriander	
1/2 teaspoon curry powder	About 2 tablespoons lemon juice

Warm oil in a heavy 3-quart pot, stir in onions and garlic. Cook, covered, over medium heat until soft and translucent, 7 to 10 minutes. Meanwhile, coarsely chop almonds in an electric blender; remove and set aside. Do same with 1/2 cup of the coconut meat. Now put remaining 1 cup of coconut meat in blender with 1 cup boiling water; whir well. Pour into a strainer set over a bowl; press coconut to extract liquid. Put coconut back in blender, add 1/2 cup boiling water and whir again; strain into first lot of coconut "milk." (The strained coconut meat is now tasteless and can be composted or offered to birds). Add coriander, curry powder and cumin to onions. Stir over medium heat for 1 minute. Stir in almonds, chopped coconut, salt and coconut "milk." Simmer uncovered 5 minutes. (Up to this point sauce can be made ahead of time, even a day or two.) Cut cod, if used, into 1-inch cubes. Add with shrimp to simmering sauce. Cover and cook over low heat 5 to 6 minutes. Fish should poach, rather than simmer. Gently stir in lemon juice and serve. Makes 4 to 5 cups. Instead of fish, 3 cups cooked drained soybeans can be heated in the sauce to make about 3 1/2 cups.

SHRIMP WITH BEAN SPROUTS AND OTHER THINGS

The preparation can be done ahead and the fresh ingredients kept chilled until cooking time.

1/4 pound boneless, skinless chicken breast	*1/2 cups sliced bamboo shoots (1/2 of an 8 ounce can)*
1/4 pound fresh mushrooms	*2 cups fresh bean sprouts (see page 00)*
About 1/2 pound Chinese celery cabbage	*1 1/2 cups chicken broth*
1/2 pound medium-sized shrimp, peeled and deveined	*1 tablespoon cornstarch*
1/4 pound skinless, boneless cod, cut into 1-inch cubes	*1 teaspoon salt*
	2 tablespoons oil

Cut chicken breast into long strips about 1/8-inch thick. Wipe mushrooms, trim a sliver off each stem, then slice thin. Cut down either side of fleshy white stalks of the celery cabbage; cut stalks into 1-inch slices and put in one pile, cut leaves into 1-inch slices and put in another. Prepare and have ready all remaining ingredients. Shortly before serving, heat oil in a 10- to 12-inch iron skillet, or in a wok. Heat should be turned up high, pan really hot. Add, all at once, shrimp, chicken breast, mushrooms, celery cabbage stalks and bamboo shoots. Cook for 2 minutes, tossing ingredients around constantly with a spoon in each hand. (This is stir-frying.) Now stir in 1 cup of chicken broth. Turn heat down a little, cover pan and let cook for 3 minutes. Stir in celery cabbage leaves and cod. Cook, covered, for 2 minutes longer; everything should be simmering merrily. Stir in bean sprouts. Quickly stir cornstarch with remaining chicken broth and salt; add to pan and stir in. Cook 30 seconds longer, then quickly tip food onto a serving dish. Serve at once. Makes 5 cups, serves about 3.

Chicken

Young and tender chicken needs only short, gentle cooking. It's an excellent source of low-fat high-quality protein with only a moderate expenditure of calories and cash. Unfortunately, the flavor of much of the chicken currently available leaves a lot to be desired. Organically raised chicken, even frozen, may occasionally be worth the extra money. If you can locate a good bird, or raise your own, there's nothing better or healthier than a simple roast or broiled chicken.

PIQUANT BROILED CHICKEN

*2 1/2 to 3 pounds chicken
  parts
1/4 cup fresh lime juice
  (lemon juice will do
  in a pinch)
1 tablespoon chopped
  garlic*

*1 teaspoon salt
1 cup thinly sliced
  onions
1/4 cup olive oil*

Rinse chicken parts and pat dry. Place in deep bowl with lime juice; turn chicken to coat each part. On a board, using the blade of a knife, mash together garlic and salt to a smooth paste. Rub this into chicken, then layer onions with chicken in bowl. Chill 1 hour. Turn each part to coat well with juice; chill 1 hour longer. Put onion rings on bottom of broiler pan. Coat chicken with oil and place on top. Broil chicken, about 8 inches from heat, 10 to 12 minutes each side. Serve with or without onion slices. Good with rice, or rice and black beans, and a salad. Or with green beans and carrots. Serves 4 or more.

SOY GINGER BAKED CHICKEN

Oven-baked chicken recipes are often made with canned soup and other high-calorie additions. Here's a delicious dish that keeps calories to a minimum.

3 pounds chicken
parts
3/4 cup white or rosé
wine
1/4 cup soy sauce
1 cup chicken broth

2 tablespoons finely
minced fresh ginger
root or 2 teaspoons
powdered ginger
1 tablespoon honey
1/4 teaspoon oregano

Rinse chicken parts and pat dry. Put in a heavy pot or casserole with remaining ingredients. Cover and bake 45 minutes at 375° F. Turn chicken pieces over, return pot to oven and cook 45 minutes longer. Serves 4 or more.

‡ CHICKEN WITH GREENS

The greens turn into a lovely sauce. If you don't have a blender, finely chop spinach and parsley before adding to pot.

2 1/2 to 3 pounds chicken
parts
1 cup water
1/2 of a 10-ounce
package frozen leaf
spinach, partially
thawed
1/4 cup parsley sprigs,
firmly pressed down
in cup to measure

1/4 cup thinly sliced
scallions
1 teaspoon dried basil
leaves
1/2 to 3/4 teaspoon salt

Put chicken in a pot in a single layer. Add the water; it should be about 1/2-inch deep. Bring to a simmer; cook, covered, for 20 minutes. Tuck spinach, parsley, scallions and basil leaves under chicken. Simmer, covered, 10 minutes longer. Lift chicken onto serving dish. Pour cooking liquid into an electric blender and whir smooth. Add 1/2 teaspoon salt, taste, add remaining salt if needed. Return chicken and sauce to pot; heat together 2 to 3 minutes without boiling. Serves 4 or more. Delicious with polenta.

This dish is also delicious made with—rabbit! Thaw 1 package (2 to 3 pounds) frozen young rabbit. Simmer for 40 minutes before adding greens.

INDIAN ROAST CHICKEN

An exotic roast chicken. Try it cold for a picnic, too. If you like, make double quantity spiced butter, freeze half for future use.

2 teaspoons coriander seeds	2 tablespoons chopped fresh ginger root
1/2 teaspoon black peppercorns	2 tablespoons butter
Seeds from 2 cardamom pods	1 chicken, weighing about 3 1/2 to 4 pounds
1 teaspoon salt	1/2 cup plain yogurt

Put coriander seeds in a mortar, suribachi or small bowl. Grind with a pestle, or end of rolling pin, until well powdered. Sift to remove husks, then grind powder with peppercorns, cardamom seeds and salt. Add chopped ginger and grind to a paste. Work in 1 tablespoon of the butter. Starting at leg end of bird, draw the skin back all the way over one leg; to do this, hold onto skin with one hand, separate skin from meat with other. (Easy to do.) With a small sharp knife make several little incisions in the leg meat; push dabs of spice mixture into them. (Don't fuss, the mixture doesn't have to be hidden neatly.) Next, expose other leg and breast meat; make incisions and dab on spice mixture. Then switch to other end of chicken and spice the wing meat. Put any remaining spice mixture inside the bird. Tie drumsticks together at tips with twine. Refrigerate bird for 1 to 2 hours, or longer if more convenient. Melt remaining butter in a deep pot; roll bird in butter then lay on one side. Cook, covered, in a 350° F. oven for 25 minutes. Turn bird over, cook 25 minutes longer. Turn breast bone up, cook, uncovered, 20 to 30 minutes longer. Spoon cooking liquid over bird 2 to 3 times. Lift bird onto dish. Spoon fat off top of cooking liquid; discard fat. Add yogurt to pot, and heat through. Serve over chicken or separately. Serves 3 to 4.

To carve chicken: with a knife, cut through joint joining thigh to main carcass. Then cut off wings in same way taking a good chunk of breast meat with them. With poultry shears, cut off the whole breast, then cut down one side of the breastbone to make 2 halves.

Lamb

Lamb is young, tender and delicious; like chicken, it should be cooked gently for just a short time. When broiled or roasted, it is best served slightly rare. Lamb steaks, cut from the leg, make an excellent cut for broiling. To flavor a roast, make tiny incisions all over a shoulder or leg before roasting, and insert slivers of garlic; or put a sprig of rosemary under it. Always serve lamb very hot; the fat is horrid lukewarm.

BASQUE LAMB STEW

This recipe came from a Basque shepherd working in the High Sierras. We did not share a common language so as he cooked, I wrote.

2 *tablespoons oil*	1/3 *cup sliced carrot*
4 *pounds neck of*	2 *cups potatoes, cut*
lamb; or 2 pounds	*like French fries*
boneless lamb	1 *teaspoon finely*
2/3 *cup water*	*chopped garlic*
1 *cup thinly sliced*	1/2 *teaspoon salt*
onions	

Heat oil in heavy 5- to 6-quart pot. Add about half the lamb and brown lightly all over; remove to a plate. Brown remaining lamb in pot. Put all lamb in pot, add water and simmer, covered, for 30 minutes. Add onions, carrot, potatoes, garlic and salt; mix in with meat. Simmer, covered, 30 minutes longer until vegetables are tender. (Some juice will come out of the lamb, but if the pot seems very dry, add another 1/4 cup of water.) One pound bone-less lamb will serve 2 to 3 persons; 2 pounds meaty neck will serve 3 persons.

‡ LAMB WITH YOGURT, CARDAMOM AND CORIANDER

If you like, prepare onion and spice mixture ahead; reheat before adding lamb.

2 cups plain yogurt	1 teaspoon ground
2 teaspoons finely	coriander
minced garlic	1/2 teaspoon ground
1 1/4 pounds boneless	black pepper
lamb, cut into	Pinch cayenne
1-inch pieces	pepper
2 tablespoons oil	1/2 teaspoon turmeric
1 cup finely chopped	2 cups green peas,
onions	fresh or frozen.
12 black cardamom	1 teaspoon salt
seeds, removed from	
white pods	

Mix yogurt and garlic in a deep bowl. Add lamb and stir to coat thoroughly. Let marinate in refrigerator for 1 hour or longer. Warm oil in a heavy 2 1/2- to 3-quart pot. Stir in onions and cook, covered, over medium heat until onions are soft, but not brown, about 5 minutes. Crush cardamom seeds in a mortar (or in a bowl with the back of a wooden spoon). Add to onion with coriander, black and cayenne peppers, and turmeric. Cook, uncovered, for 1 minute. Stir in lamb and yogurt; bring just to simmering point. Simmer, covered, over very low heat for 20 minutes. Stir in peas and salt. Simmer 3 minutes longer. Makes 4 cups. Serve as a meat sauce with rice. Good with sliced cucumbers in a sour cream dressing, or marinated carrots.

ALMOND SPICED LAMB

A beautiful example of Eastern spicing of meat. To make ahead, add almond milk, then chill. Shortly before serving, heat sauce and add lamb.

1 teaspoon coriander seeds	*1 pound boneless lamb, cut into 1/2-inch cubes*
1/2 teaspoon black peppercorns	*1/2 tablespoon finely diced fresh ginger root (optional)*
Seeds from 1 cardamom pod	
1/4 cup shelled almonds (skins on)	*1/4 teaspoon ground cloves*
1/2 cup boiling water	*1 tablespoon lemon juice*
1 cup sliced onions	
1 tablespoon butter	

Put coriander seeds in electric blender. Whir until powdered, about 30 seconds; sift onto a small piece of paper and discard husks. Put powder back in blender with peppercorns and cardamom seeds and whir until well ground; tip onto a piece of paper. Put almonds in blender container, and whir to chop them finely. Add boiling water and whir again; leave until needed. In a heavy pot, cook onion in butter for about 5 minutes over medium heat. Add lamb, ginger, cloves and ground spices; stir until meat loses its bright color, about 3 minutes. Strain liquid from almonds into pot, pressing well to extract all the liquid. Bring to a simmer, then cook, covered, for 20 minutes over very low heat. Add lemon juice and serve. Makes about 2 cups. Serves 2 to 3. Good with rice and a crunchy salad.

Almond residue, although no longer very flavorful, can be added to cookies or a cream soup, or browned in butter and used to top vegetables.

Beef

What more could be written about all-American beef, except perhaps that it's healthier for most of us to choose lean cuts more often then very fat or heavily marbled ones. As a steak, top round may require more from your teeth than filet mignon, but it has much more flavor. Buy prime or choice grades. I like to pan-broil top round because a domestic broiler can't get hot enough to really sear the outside yet keep the middle rare.

The real secret of a tender, juicy steak or roast is to let the meat do what the Frenchmen in white top hats call "repose"—rest or relax after cooking: Broil, pan-broil or roast the meat as usual. When done, remove from skillet or oven and leave for a short time in a warm place, but not so warm that the meat continues to cook. For a small steak a 5-minute rest will do the trick; a large roast needs from 15 minutes to half an hour. During this reposing period the connective tissues relax and the juices flow back into them. The result: juicier meat that cuts or carves much more easily.

ARDIE RODALE'S SUKIYAKI

1 pound top round of beef, cut in one thick slice	*3 tablespoons water*
	2 teaspoons cornstarch or arrowroot
1/2 to 3/4 pound sweet white onions	*3 tablespoons soy sauce*
1 pound sweet red or green peppers, preferably red	*1 1/2 tablespoons oil*

If possible, freeze meat until firm; it makes slicing easier. Trim off fat then cut beef across in 1/4-inch thick pieces. Slice onions into rings 1/8-inch thick. Halve peppers, discard seeds and stems; slice into long strips, 1/8-inch wide. Mix water, cornstarch, and soy sauce in small bowl. All this can be done ahead, the beef and vegetables refrigerated. Shortly before serving, heat oil in a 10- to 12-inch iron skillet or wok. Add beef slices and brown quickly on each side; meat can be rare in center. Remove to serving platter. Add vegetables and remaining oil to skillet; cook over high heat for about 30 seconds, stirring constantly. Cover skillet, lower heat and let vegetables steam until crisp-tender, about 3 minutes. (No water should be necessary, but add 1 tablespoon if you are apprehensive.) Uncover skillet, slide meat back on top of vegetables. Stir soy mixture and ȧdd to skillet. Stir over high heat for about 30 seconds until sauce is simmering and meat hot. Makes 5 to 6 cups. Serves 3 to 4. Good with rice and a salad.

BULGUR-MUSHROOM STUFFED FLANK STEAK

1/2 cup boiling water	*1/8 teaspoon marjoram*
1/4 cup coarse or	*Black pepper*
medium bulgur	*1 egg*
1/2 pound mushrooms	*1 flank steak,*
1/4 cup minced celery	*weighing 1 1/4 to 1*
1 tablespoon oil	*1/2 pounds*
1 1/2 teaspoons salt	*Watercress*
1 tablespoon chopped	
parsley	

Pour boiling water over bulgur in a bowl and let stand 10 minutes; bulgur will absorb water. Chop mushrooms finely; measure 1 cup and set aside. In a pan, sauté celery in oil for about 1 minute without browning. Add remaining mushrooms and stir over medium high heat until lightly browned, about 2 minutes. Remove pan from heat. Stir in bulgur, salt, parsley, marjoram, plenty black pepper and unbeaten egg. (Mixture will be wet.) Put flank steak flat on a board. You are going to cut a pocket in the middle. Put your left hand flat on top of meat and bend down so meat is at eye level. With a very sharp knife held parallel to the board make an incision along one long side of meat; the other three sides will remain uncut. Cut into the meat until you have a good-sized pocket; stop about 1 inch or so in from the other sides. Spoon stuffing into pocket; close the opening with two metal or wooden skewers. With a knife, lightly score a diamond pattern on top and bottom surfaces of stuffed meat, but don't cut more than 1/8-inch deep. Scoring looks pretty, and breaks up long connective tissues in meat. Set stuffed meat in a steamer basket. In a pan large enough to hold the steamer basket, bring 1 cup of water to a boil along with the 1 cup of mushrooms. Set basket in pan. Cover pan, let meat steam over medium heat for 1 1/4 to 1 1/2 hours.

Lift meat onto a board, cut in 1/2-inch thick slices. Lay slices in a circle on a platter. Put a bouquet of watercress sprigs in the center. Serve liquid from pan as a sauce. Serves 4 to 6.

ORGAN-IZED MEAT AND VEGETABLE LOAF

This juicy, nutritious, well-flavored meat loaf doesn't always cut in immaculate slices.

1/4 pound beef liver or heart	1/2 cup milk
1 pound lean ground beef, chuck or round	1/2 cup tomato juice or sauce
2 eggs plus 2 egg whites, or 4 whole eggs	1/2 pound mushrooms, finely chopped (2 1/2 cups chopped)
1 1/2 teaspoons salt	1/2 cup coarsely grated onion
1/2 teaspoon basil	1 cup coarsely grated carrot
1/2 teaspoon thyme	1 cup coarsely grated potato
2 tablespoons lemon juice	

Chop liver or heart in electric blender or meat grinder; it will be very runny. Put into a large mixing bowl. Prepare and add remaining ingredients in order given. Have ready a 9 x 5 x 3-inch loaf pan; ungreased. Now mix all ingredients together thoroughly and quickly, using a wooden spoon or one clean hand. Put mixture (about 6 1/2 cups) into loaf pan; press down lightly. If you have one, insert a meat thermometer in center of loaf. Bake 2 hours at 300° F., or until thermometer registers 170° F. Remove pan from oven, let stand 5 minutes. Put a serving platter upside down on top of loaf pan; turn the two over together. Lift pan off. Cut loaf in slices to serve. Serves 6 to 8.

BASIL SAUCE FOR PASTA (PESTO)

Here's a great reason to sow basil in your herb garden, or to buy a big bunch if you see it at the market.

>   2 cups fresh basil   1/4 cup Italian parsley
>   leaves, plucked from   leaves, if available
>   stem   2 tablespoons pignolia
>   1/4 cup oil, preferably   (pine) nuts, if
>   olive   available.·
>   1/2 teaspoon salt
>   2 teaspoons chopped
>   garlic

Wash basil leaves thoroughly and drain well. Put oil, salt and garlic in electric blender. Add 1 cup of leaves and press down. Turn on machine and whir to a smooth paste. If necessary, stop machine to push leaves down again. Add parsley, pignolia nuts and remaining basil. Press down, then whir until all are incorporated into a smooth, thick light-green mixture. Taste, add more garlic or salt if you wish. Makes about 1 cup, serves 2 to 3. Serve as a sauce for spaghetti, linguine, rice, bulgur or boiled potatoes. The recipe can be doubled or tripled, but don't double the oil; just add more as needed. With a thin layer of oil poured over the surface, pesto will keep for weeks in an airtight container in the refrigerator. It also freezes well.

Cold Main Dishes

Good nutrition is as important in warm weather as it is in cold. But as the barometer soars, our inclination to cook often sinks, and we look in the supermarket for prepared foods. What's presently available is very discouraging. Most cold cuts and canned sandwich fillings, apart from the undesirable additives they contain, are an expensive, high-fat way to buy protein. Gelatin and macaroni salads are high in calories and low in nutrients. The meat, fish and vegetable salads sold at take-out counters usually contain a larger proportion of high-calorie mayonnaise than homemade; besides they are constantly exposed to vitamin-oxidizing light and air.

If you are the supper-maker, remember it's relaxing to get organized in the cool of the morning. Prepare a Tuna Yogurt Frappé perhaps. Or poach turkey thighs or a whole chicken, and while the poultry is cooking make a curry dressing to serve with the chilled meat in the evening. While you're at it, make double the dressing and keep half to serve the next week with chilled fish or shellfish. Or put soybeans to soak before you go to bed one evening and cook them while you get breakfast the next morning. After chilling all day, they're quickly made into a protein-rich salad for supper.

Menu-makers Guide

To Start the Morning or Evening Ahead:

‡ Chicken Terrine
   Pork and Spinach Loaf
‡ Tuna Yogurt Frappé
‡ Cold Turkey with Curry Cream Dressing
‡ Chilled Whiting with Lemon Caper Dressing
   Ceviche
‡ Italian Shellfish Salad
‡ Soybean, Cabbage and Carrot Salad
   Oriental Soybean Salad

Start 30 minutes or so before serving:

Tuna Salad Niçoise

‡ CHICKEN TERRINE

A delicious "cold cut." Serve at any meal or use as a sandwich filling.

1 3/4 pounds boned, skinned chicken breast	1 3/4 teaspoons salt
1 pound ground pork	1/4 teaspoon thyme
1 cup (about 5 ounces) finely chopped cooked ham	1/4 teaspoon marjoram
	A good grating of black pepper
	2 to 4 tablespoons pistachio nuts (if available)

Grind 1 pound of the chicken breast. Cut remainder into long strips about 1/2-inch thick. Put ground chicken into a bowl with the pork, ham, salt, thyme, marjoram and pepper. Get out an 8 x 4 x 2-inch loaf pan, preferably glass. With your hands, mix the contents of the bowl together thoroughly. Put about half the mixture (2 cups) in the bottom of the loaf pan. Flatten mixture out then make a slight depression down the middle. Place chicken strips lengthwise down the depression with pistachio nuts. Press remaining chicken-pork mixture over chicken strips. Cover loaf pan tightly with foil; stick a meat therometer through foil into center of loaf. Bake for about 1 1/2 hours at 325° F., or until meat thermometer reads 185° F. Cool, then chill thoroughly. Turn terrine out onto a platter or board. Remove and discard any white fat from the jelly which will have set around the loaf. To serve, cut terrine in slices about 1/8-inch thick. Makes about 24 slices. Excellent with a hot potato or lentil salad, and either a hot vegetable or raw crunchy green salad.

PORK AND SPINACH LOAF

3 packages (10 ounces each) frozen chopped spinach, thawed, or 1 cup cooked fresh spinach	1/4 teaspoon ground sage
2 pounds ground pork	1/8 teaspoon ground mace
2 1/4 teaspoons salt	Pinch of ground cloves

Squeeze spinach in hands to extract most of water. Chop finely. Put in a bowl with remaining ingredients. Have ready an 8 x 4 x 2-inch loaf pan, preferably glass. Use one hand to work all ingredients together thoroughly. Press mixture into loaf pan. Insert a meat thermometer if you have one, in center of loaf. Bake for 1 1/2 hours at 325° F., or until thermometer registers 185° F. Cool, then chill loaf thoroughly. Turn out onto a board or platter; remove and discard creamy fat which will have solidified around loaf. Cut loaf in 1/4-inch thick slices to serve. Loaf keeps well 2 to 3 days. Good at any meal and good hot, too. Chard leaves or kale can replace spinach.

‡ TUNA YOGURT FRAPPÉ

1 cup chicken broth, canned or homemade
4 envelopes unflavored gelatin
2 cartons (8 ounces each) plain yogurt
2 cans (9 1/4 ounces each) light tuna
(drained if packed in oil)
2 tablespoons fresh lemon juice
2 tablespoons drained flat anchovy fillets (most of a 2-ounce can)

Put chicken broth in a small pan. Stir in unflavored gelatin and let soak 2 to 3 minutes. Put over low heat until dissolved and clear, 3 to 4 minutes. Let cool until needed. Put 1 carton yogurt, 1 can tuna, lemon juice and anchovy fillets in an electric blender. Whir smooth, then pour into a bowl. Add remaining yogurt and tuna to blender, whir smooth, add to bowl. Stir in the dissolved gelatin. Pour mixture into an 8 x 4- x 2-inch loaf pan, preferably glass. Chill until firm, 2 to 3 hours or longer. Loosen frappé from sides of pan then turn out onto a board or platter. Cut in 1/4-inch thick slices to serve. Makes 6 cups, 24 slices.

‡ COLD TURKEY WITH CURRY CREAM DRESSING

Turkey thighs are a thrifty buy. When poached in liquid, rather than baked, the meat is moist and tender.

2 **turkey thighs, weighing about 3 pounds total**	**Salt**
Water	**Curry Cream Dressing (recipe follows)**

Quickly pull skin off thighs and discard. Put thighs side by side in a small pot; they should fit snugly so you won't need to add a lot of water. Add just enough water to cover them. Bring to a simmer, cover, and cook over very low heat for 40 minutes. Add 2 teaspoons salt and simmer, covered, 15 minutes longer. Let thighs cool in broth; chill several hours if you can. With fingers, remove meat from bones and break it into bite-size pieces. Serve with curry dressing. Makes about 4 cups meat. Use broth for soup or stock, or in dressing.

CURRY CREAM DRESSING

1/4 **cup finely chopped onion**	2 **slices lemon, rind included**
1 1/2 **tablespoons oil**	1/4 **cup apricot, peach or pineapple preserves**
2 **tablespoons curry powder**	
1/2 **cup water or broth**	1 1/2 **cups mayonnaise**
1-**inch bay leaf**	About 2 **tablespoons lemon juice**
3/4 **teaspoon salt**	

In a small heavy pan, cook onion in oil for about 30 seconds without browning. Stir in curry powder and cook over low heat for about 2 minutes. Add water, bay leaf, 1/2 teaspoon of the salt, lemon slices and preserves. Stir, then simmer slowly, uncovered, for 10 minutes. Cool. Put mayonnaise into a bowl. Strain in about half the cooled curry mixture. Stir, add 1 tablespoon lemon juice then strain in remaining curry mixture. Add remaining 1/4 teaspoon salt and 1 tablespoon lemon juice. Taste. Dressing should have a good sweet-sour taste. Makes 1 1/2 cups. Chill before using.

This mild delicate sauce is one of my favorites. Serve it also with cold chicken, hard-cooked eggs or cold flaked fish. It can be used as a dressing for fruit. Refrigerated in an airtight container, it will keep for weeks.

‡ CHILLED WHITING WITH LEMON CAPER DRESSING

1 1/2 pounds of whiting,
weighed with heads
and tails removed,
or other white,
non-oily fish, or 1
pound any white

fish fillet such as
cod, scrod or
flounder
Lemon Caper
Dressing (recipe
follows)

Put fish in a steamer basket and set over 1/2-inch of simmering water in a pan. Cover pan and let simmer until fish is just cooked, 10 to 12 minutes. Remove from pan. (Fish should be opalescent, white and just soft to the touch.) When cool enough to handle, use fingers to flake fish and remove all skin and bones. Serve fish warm or chilled; mound it on lettuce leaves and serve the sauce separately. This is an excellent way to use the least expensive white fish available. Makes about 2 cups cooked flaked fish.

LEMON CAPER DRESSING

1 can (2 ounces) flat
anchovy fillets, well
drained
1/2 cup coarsely
chopped scallions or
shallots
1/4 cup capers, rinsed
and drained

1 cup parsley sprigs,
firmly pressed down
in cup to measure
1/3 cup lemon juice
1 cup olive oil
1 teaspoon salt

Put all ingredients in electric blender and whir smooth. Makes 2 cups. This sauce keeps for several days in the refrigerator and is excellent with cold fish, beef, poultry, cooked navy or soybeans, canned mackerel or tuna.

CEVICHE

*2/3 cup lime juice, or
half lemon juice,
half lime
1/2 teaspoon minced
garlic
1/2 teaspoon salt*

*About 8 wafer-thin slices
of sweet onion
A good grating of black
pepper
1 pound fillet of sole,
flounder or other
white fish*

Mix lime juice, garlic, salt, onion and black pepper in a bowl. Cut fish into strips about 2-inches long, 1/4-inch wide. Mix with seasoned lime juice. Juice should just cover fish, add more if it does not. Cover and refrigerate for at least 3 hours, but up to 24 hours if you wish. The lime juice "cooks" the fish; no heat is applied. When ready the fish will be quite white all the way through and will look and taste cooked. Makes about 2 cups. Serve with hot steamed corn and potatoes. Ceviche can be served as an appetizer by itself, or spooned into avocado halves. Sometimes chopped avocado and tomatoes are added just before serving.

‡ ITALIAN SHELLFISH SALAD

Although untraditional in Italy, where this recipe originated, you can add steamed chunks of cod or haddock to the shellfish. Squid is very inexpensive and tastes something like lobster.

1/2 pound medium-sized shrimp, peeled and deveined
1/2 pound scallops
1 pound squid
2 pounds cherrystone clams, scrubbed
3/4 cup olive oil
3 tablespoons cider vinegar
1 1/2 tablespoons Dijon-style mustard
1 teaspoon chopped garlic
1/2 teaspoon salt
1 tablespoon chopped parsley
2 tablespoons rinsed capers

Put scallops and shrimp in a steamer basket over 1/2-inch of boiling water in a pan. Let cook, covered, over medium heat for 5 minutes. When cooked, remove from basket and cool. Meanwhile, prepare the squid: pull off tentacles from just in front of eyes. With fingers, clean out the sac and remove the plasticlike backbone from inside. Quickly wash tentacles and sac, rubbing off any black skin with your fingers. Steam squid (no need to change water) until white and tender, about 10 minutes. Cool. Cut sac into 1/2-inch circles; leave tentacles whole. Meanwhile, using same pan, steam clams until shells open, 6 to 8 minutes. Remove from shells. Put all remaining ingredients in a bowl and mix well with a small whisk. Stir in the scallops (sliced if large), shrimp, squid and clams. Chill for at least 6 hours before serving. Yields 5 cups cooked seafood.

TUNA SALAD NICOISE

A fresh and delicious change from mayonnaise-dressed salads.

1/2 pound green beans, trimmed and cut into 1-inch pieces
1 pound ripe tomatoes, round, plum or cherry
1 cucumber, peeled and cut into 1/2-inch chunks
1/4 teaspoon salt
Plenty black pepper
1 tablespoon cider vinegar

3 tablespoons oil
2 tablespoons chopped fresh herbs such as parsley, chives, savory, and thyme, if available
2 cans (7 ounces each) tuna, well drained
About 8 flat anchovy fillets (part of a 2-ounce can)
6 pitted black olives, cut in halves

Put beans in a steamer basket in a pan over 1/2-inch of boiling water. Cover pan and cook over medium heat until beans are crisp-tender, about 5 minutes. Remove from pan and cool. Add tomatoes all at once to a pan of boiling water; count to 10 slowly. Immediately pour off boiling water and fill pan with cold to stop tomatoes cooking. Peel skin off tomatoes (a bore with cherry tomatoes, but worth it). Leave cherry tomatoes whole, cut larger ones into eighths. Put in serving dish with beans and cucumber. Whisk salt, pepper, cider vinegar, oil and herbs in a small bowl. Pour over vegetables and toss gently. (You can chill salad for 30 to 60 minutes if you wish). Break tuna in chunks and put on top of vegetables. Cut anchovy fillets in half lengthwise and use to make a lattice decoration on top of the tuna. Put olive halves, cut side down, inside the lattice. At serving time, gently toss the whole salad. Makes 6 cups, serves 4. Although olives and anchovies are what "Niçoise" is all about, the salad is still good without them.

‡ SOYBEAN, CABBAGE, AND CARROT SALAD

A filling, no-meat main dish.

1 cup dried soybeans; or 2 1/2 cups cooked soybeans	2 teaspoons lemon juice
1/3 cup yogurt	1 cup shredded cabbage
1/3 cup mayonnaise	1/2 cup coarsely grated carrot
1/2 teaspoon salt	
1/2 teaspoon Dijon-style mustard	

If using dried beans soak them in 4 cups water for 8 to 24 hours in refrigerator. Rinse, put in pan with fresh cold water, bring to a boil and simmer, covered for 1 1/2 to 2 hours. Drain and cool. In serving bowl, mix yogurt, mayonnaise, salt, mustard and lemon juice. Shred cabbage, using a knife or shredder. Add with carrots and beans to dressing in bowl. Toss lightly to mix. Serve at once or chill for 30 minutes. Makes 3 1/2 cups.

ORIENTAL SOYBEAN SALAD

1 cup dried soybeans; or 2 1/2 cups cooked soybeans	1 teaspoon finely minced fresh gingerroot
1/4 cup rice or cider vinegar	1/2 cup grated carrot; or 1/2 cup fresh mung bean sprouts*
1 tablespoon honey	1/2 cup shredded cabbage or zucchini
1 1/2 tablespoons finely sliced scallions	
1/2 teaspoon salt	

If using dried soybeans, soak them in the refrigerator in 4 cups water for 8 to 24 hours. Rinse, put in pan with fresh cold water. Bring to a boil, simmer, covered, 1 1/2 to 2 hours. Drain and cool. In a serving bowl, mix vinegar, honey, scallions, salt and ginger. Mix in drained, cooked soybeans. Add carrot or bean

If using mung bean sprouts, steam them for 1 minute in a steamer basket over boiling water.

sprouts, and cabbage or zucchini, to soybeans and dressing. Mix all together lightly. Serve at once or chill for 30 minutes. Makes 3 cups.

Meat-Free Main Dishes

A number of people are forsaking the 16-ounce sirloin and turning to complete or partial vegetarianism. It is true that some Americans may be eating a great deal more meat than their bodies need or can use as protein. But a vegetarian diet, particularly one that excludes even milk and eggs, requires considerable knowledge and skill to put together. It should not be undertaken lightly. You don't have to be a vegetarian to enjoy a meat-free meal now and then; it can make a pleasant change and be economical too, as the following recipes show.

Menu-maker's Guide

Thirty Minutes or Less from Start to Finish:

‡ Vegetables au Gratin
Bean Curd and Vegetables in Soy Ginger Sauce
Chanchonka

More than Thirty Minutes:

‡ Soybean Moussaka (beans ahead, then 2 hours)
Rice, Cabbage, Beans and Cheese (rice, beans ahead, 15 minutes to finish)
Kichri (1 hour and 15 minutes)
‡ Falafel (soak chick peas, then 45 minutes to finish)

‡ VEGETABLES AU GRATIN

Infusing milk with vegetables and herbs imparts a very special flavor to the sauce.

2 cups milk
1 cup mixed sliced
   celery, carrot and
   onion, for flavoring
1 1-inch bay leaf
6 peppercorns
   Pinch thyme
1/4 cup soft butter; or 3
   tablespoons oil
1/4 cup unbleached
   white flour or
   whole-wheat pastry
   flour

1 teaspoon salt
1 cup grated sharp
   Cheddar cheese
6 cups freshly steamed
   vegetables such as
   sliced carrots,
   cauliflower sprigs
   and peas

Heat milk with the 1 cup sliced vegetables, bay leaf, pepper-corns and thyme in a heavy 2- to 3-quart pot. Cover and let barely simmer until milk is well flavored, 10 to 15 minutes. (Use this time to steam the vegetables). Remove milk from stove, cool 2 to 3 minutes. Lift out flavorings with a slotted spoon. Mix butter (or oil) with flour in a small bowl; whisk into milk about 1 tablespoon at a time. When smooth, put pot back on stove and whisk sauce until simmering. Simmer over very low heat for 3 minutes to cook flour. Add salt, taste to check seasoning. Mix sauce with hot vegetables. Spoon into a shallow baking dish, sprinkle with grated cheese. Broil about 2 minutes until cheese is melted and slightly brown. Makes 6 cups. Serves 4 or more. Try also with Brussels sprouts and cauliflower sprigs; summer squash, potatoes and corn; mushrooms, potatoes and green beans.

BEAN CURD AND VEGETABLES IN SOY GINGER SAUCE

2 *tablespoons oil*
1-1/2 cups carrots, cut
  into diagonal
  1/2-inch slices
1-1/2 cups onion rings,
  1/8-inch thick
1 cup celery, cut into
  diagonal 1/2-inch
  slices
1/2 cup water

2 *tablespoons soy*
  sauce
2 *teaspoons grated or*
  finely minced fresh
  ginger root
3 *teaspoons cornstarch*
1 to 2 cups canned or
  fresh bean curd, cut
  into 1/2-inch
  squares

Warm oil in heavy 4- to 6-quart pot. Add cut-up vegetables and with a spoon in each hand, toss them over medium high heat for 3 minutes. Add water, toss again briefly; cover and cook over medium high heat, 7 to 10 minutes, until vegetables are crisp-tender. Meanwhile, mix soy sauce, ginger and cornstarch in a small bowl. When vegetables are ready, add bean curd. Stir up soy sauce mixture and add to pot. Stir over heat until simmering. Serve with brown rice or bulgur. Makes about 4 1/2 cups. Try also with peeled sweet potato chunks, beansprouts and cooked chestnuts; lotus root, bamboo shoots and water chestnuts.

CHANCHONKA—Eggplant, Peppers and Onions

If skins are harsh, peppers can be broiled (see page 116), peeled, and added to onions with eggplant. This is a native dish of Iraq.

1 eggplant, about 1
  1/2 pounds
3/4 pound sweet white
  onions
1 pound sweet red
  peppers
1 pound sweet green
  peppers
2 *teaspoons chopped*
  garlic

2 *teaspoons salt*
2/3 cup oil, part olive
  oil if you wish
  Pinch thyme
  2-inch bay leaf
1/3 cup water
1/4 cup cider or wine
  vinegar
Plenty black pepper

Wash eggplant but do not peel or cut. Broil for 10 to 15 minutes until tender, turning every 3 to 4 minutes. Pierce center with a skewer to test; it should feel soft. When done, remove eggplant from broiler; it will collapse as it cools. Meanwhile, slice onions 1/8-inch thick. Halve peppers, discard stem and seeds, cut into 1/4-inch strips. With the blade of a knife crush garlic with salt to a smooth paste on a board. Heat half the oil in a heavy 5- to 6-quart pot. Stir in onions, peppers, garlic, thyme, bay leaf and water. Cook, covered, over medium heat 15 to 20 minutes; stir once or twice. When done, vegetables should be crisp-tender, but not brown. Meanwhile, cut eggplant (with skin left on) into 1-inch cubes. Add to pot, cover and cook over low heat 4 to 5 minutes. Mix in remaining oil, the vinegar, and pepper. Serve warm or cold as a main dish or salad. Makes about 6 cups. Keeps several days if refrigerated.

When vegetables are plentiful try this: make double quantity but add vinegar to only half. For a second meal, spread the chanchonka without vinegar in a fireproof dish. Make 6 hollows in surface and break an egg into each. Bake 15 to 20 minutes at 325° F. just until eggs are set. Serve for lunch, supper or breakfast.

‡ SOYBEAN MOUSSAKA

2 1/2 cups cooked soybeans or 1 cup dried soybeans	1/4 teaspoon oregano
	2 teaspoons salt
2 eggplants, each weighing about 1 pound	1 teaspoon minced garlic
Oil	1 can (6 ounces) tomato paste
3/4 cup finely chopped onion	3 eggs
1/4 teaspoon thyme	2 cups shredded sharp Cheddar, or Muenster, cheese

If using dried beans, soak them in refrigerator in 4 cups water for 8 to 24 hours. Rinse, put in pan, cover with fresh cold water, bring to a simmer and cook, covered, 1 1/2 to 2 hours; this can be done ahead. About 1 1/2 hours before serving, wipe eggplants but do not peel. Cut off stems and cut each eggplant in four parts lengthwise. Brush all over with oil and set on a baking tray. Bake at 400° F. until tender, 20 to 25 minutes. When eggplant is cool enough to handle, carefully scrape meat off skins, leaving skins intact. Chop eggplant meat coarsely and set aside. Line a straight-sided 6-cup dish with skins: put pointed ends toward center, let other ends hang over the edge. Heat 1 tablespoon oil in a heavy 2 1/2- to 3-quart pot. Stir in onion. Cook, covered, over medium heat until soft, about 5 minutes. Uncover, cook 5 to 7 minutes longer until golden; stir now and then. Stir in the chopped eggplant and the cooked, drained soybeans. Let heat through while you stir in the thyme, oregano, salt, garlic and tomato paste. When warm, remove pot from heat; beat in eggs one at a time. Put about 1/3 of mixture into dish lined with eggplant skins. Top with 1 cup cheese. Add another 1/3 of eggplant, then remaining cheese. Finish with last 1/3 of eggplant. Fold loose skins over top of moussaka. Bake 30 minutes at 350° F.; turn heat down to 325° F. and bake 15 minutes longer. Let stand 10 minutes. Put serving plate on top of Moussaka, invert both together. Lift dish off. To serve, cut in wedges with sharp, pointed knife. Makes about 5 1/2 cups, serves 6 or more. Excellent cold, too.

RICE, CABBAGE, BEANS AND CHEESE

1 cup dried red kidney beans; or 2–1/2 cups cooked beans
Water
Salt
1/2 cup uncooked brown rice; or 1 cup cooked brown rice
1 small cabbage, about 1 to 1 1/2 pounds (4 to 5 cups shredded)

1/4 cup (1/2 stick) butter
1 teaspoon dried sage
1 cup grated sharp Cheddar or Switzerland Swiss cheese
Pepper to taste

Soak *dried* beans in 3 cups water 8 to 24 hours in refrigerator. Bring to boil, add 1 teaspoon salt and simmer covered 1 1/2 hours. If starting with *uncooked* rice, bring 1 1/2 cups water to a boil in a small pot, add rice and 1/2 teaspoon salt. Simmer covered, about 40 minutes, until rice is tender and water is absorbed. Rice and beans can both be prepared ahead. Shortly before serving, shred cabbage with a knife. Put in steamer basket set in a pan over 1/2-inch boiling water. Cover pan and let cabbage steam just until tender, 5 to 7 minutes. Meanwhile, melt butter in large heavy pot; crumble sage with fingers, add to butter and leave over low heat 2 to 3 minutes. Add rice and cabbage, toss gently to mix. Add cheese and toss again. Taste mixture, add black pepper and more salt if needed. Add drained beans and warm through, 3 to 4 minutes. Makes about 4 1/2 cups. Serves 3 or more.

KICHRI

People of India serve kichri as a meatless main dish, or as an accompaniment to meat.

8 whole allspice	1/2 cup chopped onion
9 black peppercorns	1/3 cup brown rice
Seeds from 2 cardamom pods	1 teaspoon salt
1/8 teaspoon ground cloves	1 tablespoon lemon juice
1 tablespoon butter or oil	3 cups water
	1/3 cup brown lentils

Grind the allspice, peppercorns and cardamom seeds to a powder in a mortar; or use the end of a rolling pin in a small bowl. When ground, add cloves. Melt butter in a small heavy pot; stir in onion. Cook, covered, over medium heat for 3 minutes. Add rice and stir over medium heat for a few seconds. Stir in ground spices and salt, then lemon juice and water. Simmer, covered over medium heat for 20 minutes. Stir in lentils and cook just until tender, 20 to 25 minutes longer. Makes 2 cups. Serves 2. Good with sliced cucumbers dressed with salt, mint and yogurt.

‡ FALAFEL—Chick Pea Croquettes

Falafel can be served as a main dish, as snack or hors d'oeuvres. Syrians put 3 to 4 inside pita bread to make a sandwich, along with shredded lettuce, tomato slices and Taratoor Sauce (recipe follows). The batter freezes well and is convenient to have on hand.

1 cup dried chick peas	1/4 cup lemon juice
Cold water	1 1/2 teaspoons salt
6 stalks parsley (stems and leaves), or cilantro (cilantro is fresh coriander)	1/2 teaspoon ground cumin
	1/4 teaspoon black pepper
1/2 cup chopped onion (use scallions with cilantro)	1/4 teaspoon dried basil
	Oil for frying (soy or corn)
2 teaspoons chopped garlic	

Soak chick peas in 4 cups cold water in refrigerator for 8 to 24 hours. Drain and put through meat grinder (use finest blade if you have a choice) along with parsley, onion and garlic. Mix with lemon juice, salt, cumin, pepper, basil and 2 tablespoons water. (This can be done ahead.) To cook falafel, heat about 2 inches of oil in a deep pan (to prevent overflow). Scoop up mixture in rounded tablespoons, form into balls and lower into oil. (Or, scoop up mixture with a small ice-cream scoop and put directly into oil.) Don't try to cook more than one layer at a time. Fry until cooked through and brown, about 4 minutes. Lift out one with a spoon and check center is no longer soft. If falafel are not submerged in oil, turn once while cooking. When done, lift out with slotted spoon and drain thoroughly on paper. Serve hot. Makes 18 to 20. Note: falafel absorb practically no oil while cooking.

TARATOOR SAUCE

1/3 cup canned sesame
tahini
1/3 cup cold water
1 teaspoon salt

1/2 teaspoon chopped
garlic
1/2 cup lemon juice

Spoon tahini into a bowl; whisk water in 1 tablespoon at a time. On a board with the blade of a knife, crush garlic and salt to a smooth paste. Add to tahini. Whisk in lemon juice 1 tablespoonful at a time. Sauce will turn pale and thin. Makes about 1 cup. If you double the recipe, you can use an electric blender, and add garlic and salt without crushing.

5

How to Cook Fresh Vegetables

Vegetables look their prettiest, taste their best and retain as many nutrients as possible when served undercooked, rather than overcooked. Some vegetables, such as carrots, beets and rutabagas, are actually better cooked than raw because cooking breaks up tough fibres and makes certain nutrients more available.

If you have anti-vegetable children, you may be able to interest them more easily in raw vegetables than cooked ones. Cauliflower for instance, broken into tiny flowerets, and served raw with a Russian-type dressing or favorite dip, often captures the interest of a child who won't have anything to do with it cooked.

I like vegetables cooked very simply, so that their true flavors come through. They are best cooked in a minimum of liquid or steamed in a steamer basket. Green vegetables such as cabbage should be cooked at a medium temperature otherwise they develop that terrible "cabbagey" taste and smell. Use any liquid left from cooking vegetables if you can; add it to a soup or sauce, or simply drink it later. It makes a refreshing beverage for the cook.

Over a period of time eat many different vegetables. But be sure to emphasize those from the group especially high in vitamins A or C (see introduction) and keep the following points in mind:

1. Buy really fresh looking green vegetables. Tired, wilted ones may have suffered considerable vitamin loss.

2. Store green vegetables, summer squash, carrots and beets in the refrigerator. Keep onions, potatoes and winter squash cool, but do not refrigerate.

3. Wash vegetables quickly, and before cutting them up. Don't soak for hours in water.

4. Peel vegetables thinly and cut them up as close to cooking time as possible. If they must wait, cover and chill them.

5. Generally, the less you cut up vegetables the less the loss of nutrients. If you're steaming potatoes, for instance, steam them whole with their skins on.

6. Don't add baking soda to cooking water; it destroys vitamins.

7. To conserve nutrients, use a covered pan where possible and preferably not glass.

8. Use frozen and canned vegetables, too, between seasons to add variety to the diet, to increase the consumption of vegetables, and when fresh produce is unripe or of poor quality.

Menu-Makers Guide

Green, deep yellow and leafy vegetables

‡ Skillet Broccoli
‡ Carrots Vichy
　Chard Italian Style
　Collard Greens with Bacon
　Dandelion Parmesan
　String Beans, Indian Style
　Green Peppers Baked with Cheese
　Green Tomato Casserole
‡ Basic Kale
　Acorn Squash
　Sweet Potatoes and Yams

Legumes to use where extra protein is needed

　Black Beans Cubano
　Spanish Lentils

Mixed Vegetable Dishes

Eggplant, Tomatoes and Cream
Tomatoes, Corn and Peppers
‡ Zucchini, Tomatoes and Mushrooms

Other Vegetables which supply many nutrients, but are not outstanding sources of vitamins A and C

‡ Jerusalem Artichokes Velouté
Sweet and Sour Beets
Celeriac in Lemon Broth
Corn Pudding
Minted Cucumbers
‡ Broiled Herbed Eggplant
Mushroom Ragout
Creamed Potatoes
Rutabaga-Potato Purée
Rutabaga Pancakes
Turnips with Sour Cream and Horseradish
Dilled Zucchini

‡ JERUSALEM ARTICHOKES VELOUTÉ

Look for these in health food stores and farm markets. They are a root vegetable, quite different from green globe artichokes.

1 pound Jerusalem artichokes (about 3 cups cut up)	*1 tablespoon unbleached white flour*
Water	*1/2 cup milk or light cream*
3/4 teaspoon salt	
1 tablespoon butter	

Scrub artichokes with a brush, rinse well, and cut into fairly large chunks. Put in a pot, add water to cover (about 1 1/2 cups) and salt. Bring to a simmer, cover and cook until just tender, 15 to 20 minutes. Lift out artichokes with a splotted spoon. Turn up heat and boil liquid until 1/2 cup remains. With a knife, mash butter and flour to a smooth paste on a plate. Remove pot from heat, let cool 1 minute then whisk in the butter/flour paste. When smooth, return to heat, bring to a simmer and add milk or cream. Let cook 3 to 4 minutes. Taste to check seasoning. Put artichokes back in sauce and heat through. Serves 4. Good alone, or with beef or chicken or lamb.

Variation: add 2 tomatoes, peeled, seeded and cut into pieces just before serving.

BLACK BEANS CUBANO

1 cup black beans	*1/3 cup minced onion*
3 cups water	*1/4 teaspoon oregano*
2-inch bay leaf	*1/4 teaspoon ground*
1/4 cup olive oil	*cumin*
1/2 teaspoon chopped	*1 teaspoon wine*
garlic	*vinegar (Spanish*
1 teaspoon salt	*Sherry wine vinegar*
1/2 cup minced sweet	*is particularly*
red or green pepper	*delicious)*

Soak beans in water for 8 to 24 hours in refrigerator. Bring to boil (in same water), add bay leaf and simmer, covered, for 1 hour. Meanwhile, warm oil in a small pan. Add remaining ingredients, except for wine vinegar, and cook over low heat for 10 minutes until vegetables are soft but not brown. Stir often. Add to beans and simmer, covered, 1 hour longer. Add vinegar and serve. Makes about 3 cups. Excellent with pork.

SWEET-AND-SOUR BEETS

1 cup water	*2 teaspoons cornstarch*
1 pound beets, peeled	*4 teaspoons honey*
and cut into	*1/4 cup cider vinegar*
1/4-inch cubes	*1/2 teaspoon salt*

Bring water to boil in a small heavy pot. Stir in beets, reduce heat and simmer, covered, over medium heat until tender, about

15 minutes. Mix remaining ingredients in a small bowl, stir into beets and simmer, covered, for 2 minutes before serving. Makes about 3 cups. Reheats well. Good with beef.

‡ SKILLET BROCCOLI

1 bunch broccoli   *1 teaspoon butter*
Water   *1/2 teaspoon salt*

Cut off and discard about 2 inches from bottom of each stalk of broccoli. Cut remaining thick stalk into 1-inch chunks. Rinse, and put into a lidded 8-inch skillet with about 1/4 inch of water. Bring to a simmer then cook, covered, for about four minutes. Rinse broccoli flowers, add to skillet with butter and salt. Cook covered, just until stems feel tender when pierced with a knife, about 5 to 8 minutes. Serve with any remaining liquid in pan. Makes about 4 cups, serves 4 to 6.

‡ CARROTS VICHY

1 pound carrots,   *3/4 teaspoon salt*
*   peeled or just*   *1 tablespoon chopped*
*   scrubbed*   *   parsley (optional)*
1 1/2 to 2 tablespoons   *Water*
*   butter*

Slice carrots thinly (about 1/16 inch). Put in a small heavy pot with butter, salt, and about 1/4 inch of water. Bring quickly to boil, cover, and simmer over a low flame until carrots are tender, about 7 minutes. Shake pot once or twice. Remove lid, turn up heat and let boil fast until any remaining liquid has practically disappeared, about 2 minutes. Carrots will be shiny. Mix in parsley gently and serve. Makes about 3 cups.

CELERIAC IN LEMON BROTH

*1 celeriac, weighing
about 1 pound (3
cups cut up)
1 cup chicken broth
1 tablespoon lemon
juice*

*1 teaspoon butter
1 tablespoon chopped
parsley or chives*

Cut the fringe of small roots off celeriac and discard. Peel celeriac, rinse quickly and cut into 1/2-inch chunks. Bring to boil in a small pot with chicken broth and lemon juice. Reduce heat, cover and simmer until tender, about 15 minutes. Lift out celeriac with a slotted spoon. Boil liquid fast until 1/4 cup remains, about 2 minutes. Turn heat to low. Gently mix in the celeriac, butter, and parsley or chives. Makes about 2 cups. Serve with pork, game or turkey.

CHARD

Chard grows about 18-inches high and has dark green leaves with gleaming white stems. Buy it only when it looks very clean and fresh. The following recipe uses both stems and leaves, but it's more fun to cook the leaves alone this way, and use the stems for another meal. Cook them Chinese-style, or steam and serve with brown butter or a cheese sauce.

CHARD ITALIAN STYLE

*1 bunch (11 ounces)
chard
1 tablespoon olive oil
1/2 teaspoon minced
garlic*

*1/4 teaspoon salt
Some black pepper
1/2 tablespoon pignolia
(pine) nuts
(optional)*

Check weight of chard when buying, as size of bunches vary considerably; adapt recipe if necessary. Remove stems at the point where the leaves begin. Rinse stems and cut into 1-inch pieces. Wash leaves quickly and shake off much of the water. Warm oil in a heavy 2- to 3-quart pot; add stems and garlic and cook over medium heat 1 to 2 minutes. Turn up heat, add leaves and stir around slowly until they are hot, about 1 minute. Lower heat, cover pot, and let leaves steam until tender, 5 to 7 minutes. Stir in salt, pepper and pignolia nuts. Taste to check for tenderness and seasoning. Makes about 1 cup.

COLLARD GREENS WITH BACON

1 bunch collard greens, weighing about 1 1/2 pounds
6 strips bacon, diced; or 1/3 cup finely diced salt pork

1/4 cup water
Black pepper

Collard greens come in clumps; trim off root end to break up. Pick off and discard all hard stems. Wash greens quickly in two waters and drain. Cook the bacon or salt pork in a large heavy pot until crisp. Pour off all but 2 to 3 tablespoons fat. Turn up heat, add greens and water. Stir slowly for about 2 minutes until leaves are hot and wilting. Turn down heat, cover pot and let greens cook over medium heat until tender, 10 minutes or longer. Add black pepper to taste and serve. Makes about 4 cups. Do not discard liquid; drink or dip bread into it.

CORN PUDDING

A cross between a pudding and a custard.

1 teaspoon butter
4 eggs
2 cups milk; or 1 cup each milk and light cream

1 teaspoon salt
A good grating of pepper
4 to 6 ears of corn

Rub butter on inside of a 1 1/2-quart baking dish. Whisk eggs in a bowl, then stir in milk, salt and pepper. Husk 3 to 4 ears of the corn and grate on a coarse grater. Grate each husk enough so milky part comes out of cob. Grate enough ears of corn to make 2 cups pulp. Stir into egg mixture. Pour into buttered baking dish. Set dish in another larger pan, such as a roasting pan, and fill the larger pan with water to 1 inch below top of corn mixture. Put in oven and bake at 350° F. until set, 50 to 70 minutes. When done, center should be firm, not liquid. Makes about 4 1/2 cups. Delicious with ham.

MINTED CUCUMBERS

When your garden is overflowing with cucumbers and you want a change from salad.

1 cucumber	*Pinch dried mint*
1 tablespoon butter	*leaves; or about 1*
1/4 teaspoon salt	*teaspoon chopped*
1 teaspoon lemon	*fresh mint*
juice	

Peel cucumber, cut into 6 slices lengthwise then across into 1-inch chunks. Melt butter in a small heavy pot; stir in cucumber. Cover and cook over low heat for 5 minutes without browning. Stir in salt, lemon juice and mint. Cover and cook 2 minutes longer. Cucumber should be tender and slightly translucent. Makes about 1 3/4 cups. Good with salmon or lamb.

DANDELION GREENS

Sold in two ways—young and tender for salad, more mature for cooking. The flavor is somewhat bitter, so serve only a small portion, 1/4 cup per person.

DANDELION PARMESAN

1 bunch dandelion leaves, weighing 10 to 11 ounces	*2 tablespoons grated fresh Parmesan cheese*
2 tablespoons olive oil	*1/4 teaspoon salt*
1 teaspoon minced garlic	

Remove and discard tough stems from dandelions. Wash quickly in two waters and drain. Leave whole, or cut into pieces. Warm oil in a heavy pot, add garlic and cook for about 1 minute. Turn up heat, add leaves and stir slowly until leaves are hot and wilting. Lower heat, cover pot and let cook 10 to 15 minutes longer. Stir in Parmesan cheese and salt. Makes about 1 cup. Good with veal or beef.

‡ BROILED HERBED EGGPLANT

*When fried in a skillet, eggplant **drinks up** oil. This way, **you** control the amount of oil.*

1/4 cup olive oil	*1 eggplant, weighing about 1 1/2 pounds*
1/8 teaspoon each basil, thyme, oregano	*2 tablespoons butter*
1 teaspoon salt	*1 tablespoon chopped parsley*
Plenty black pepper	
1/2 teaspoon minced garlic	*1/4 cup breadcrumbs, fresh or dried*

In a small pan, mix olive oil, herbs, salt, pepper and garlic. Wipe eggplant, trim off stem, and cut into 8 round slices. Brush slices on both sides with the oil-herb mixture; lay on a cookie sheet. Bake for 15 minutes at 375° F., then turn slices over and bake 15 minutes longer. Melt butter in oil-herb pan; stir in parsley and breadcrumbs. Spoon over top of each eggplant slice. Broil until brown, 2 to 3 minutes. Serves 4.

EGGPLANT, TOMATOES AND CREAM

*1 eggplant, weighing
　about 2 pounds
Olive oil
2 tablespoons butter
3/4 cup chopped onions
1 1/2 pounds red, ripe
　tomatoes*

*1 cup light cream
4 teaspoons cornstarch
1 1/4 teaspoons salt
3/4 cup grated
　Switzerland Swiss
　cheese*

Wipe eggplant, discard stem, and cut into 1/2-inch rounds. Brush each slice lightly with olive oil and set on a cookie sheet. Broil 5 minutes each side. Melt butter in a heavy skillet, stir in onions; cook, covered, over medium heat until slightly soft, about 2 minutes. Uncover and let brown slowly, 5 to 7 minutes longer. Meanwhile, bring a pan of water to a boil. Add tomatoes, count slowly to 10, then pour off water and fill pan with cold water to stop cooking; peel off skins, cut in slices about 1/8-inch thick. Add half the tomato slices at a time to the onions and cook for two minutes each side. Now layer tomatoes and onion with eggplant in a 2-quart baking dish. Mix cream with cornstarch and salt; pour over vegetables. Top with grated cheese. Bake for 20 minutes at 375° F. Serves 6. Serve as a first course, as an accompaniment, or as a vegetable main dish.

STRING BEANS, INDIAN STYLE

String beans are also excellent when trimmed, left whole, steamed for about 7 minutes, then dressed with butter, salt and pepper.

*2 tablespoons oil
1 1/2 teaspoons mustard
　seeds
3/4 cup coarsely
　chopped onions
1 pound green beans,
　fresh or frozen*

*1/2 teaspoon ground
　cumin seed
3/4 teaspoon salt
1/2 teaspoon tumeric
1 tablespoon lemon
　juice*

Heat oil in a heavy 2- to 3- quart pot, add mustard seed and cook until black, about 3 minutes. Stir in onion and cook slowly until golden, 10 to 15 minutes. Meanwhile trim ends off fresh green beans, and cut into 1/4-inch pieces. Let frozen beans thaw a little. When onions are ready, stir in cumin, salt, tumeric, lemon juice and beans. Cook covered over medium heat until beans are crisp-tender, 15 to 20 minutes. Stir frequently. Add 1 tablespoon water only if beans start to stick. Makes 3 cups. Good with chicken or lamb.

GREEN PEPPERS BAKED WITH CHEESE

Make this with regular green peppers or the long pale type called "fryers."

4 large green peppers,	*Salt*
or fryers	*Black pepper*
Olive oil	
1/2 cup grated sharp	
Cheddar cheese	

Halve peppers and remove seeds. Brush insides and cut surface very lightly with oil. Lay pepper halves, skin side down, in a baking dish. Sprinkle grated cheese inside each half and sprinkle lightly with salt and pepper. Bake at 400° F. just until peppers are tender, about 30 minutes, 20 minutes for fryers. Serves 4 or more.

GREEN TOMATO CASSEROLE

5 green tomatoes	*Black pepper*
(about 1 3/4	*2 cups (4 ounces)*
pounds)	*grated sharp*
Butter	*Cheddar cheese*
Salt	

Halve the tomatoes and cut out any white core. Lay cut side down on a board and slice 1/4-inch thick. Lightly butter a 5-cup baking dish. Put about 1/3 of tomato slices in bottom of dish, sprinkle with about 1/8 teaspoon salt, some pepper, and about 1/3 of the cheese. Repeat with remaining ingredients. Top with 1 tablespoon butter cut into little pieces. Cover dish and bake at 400° F. for 45 minutes. If tomatoes are not tender, bake 10 to 15 minutes longer. Serves 6.

‡ BASIC KALE

Dark green curly leaves with a delicious flavor. If the flavor is too strong for your taste, simmer the leaves for 1 minute in plenty of water. Drain thoroughly, then heat through in the seasoned butter. Of course you do lose some vitamins, but if it helps develop a taste for kale, it's worth it.

1 bunch (1 pound) kale	*2/3 cup diced green pepper*
2 tablespoons butter	*1/2 teaspoon salt*
1/3 cup finely chopped onion	*Black pepper*

Remove and discard tough stems from kale. Wash leaves in two waters and drain, shake off much of the water. Leave leaves whole, or cut into 2-inch pieces. Melt butter in a large heavy pot. Stir in onion and green pepper; cover and cook over low heat until soft, about 2 minutes. Turn up heat, add kale and stir slowly for about 1 minute until hot. Lower heat, cover pot, and let cook just until tender, 5 to 7 minutes. Stir in salt, and pepper. Makes about 2 cups. Good alone, or with any meat.

SPANISH LENTILS

1 tablespoon oil	*2 cups water*
2 tablespoons finely chopped onion	*Pinch oregano*
2 tablespoons finely chopped green pepper	*1 teaspoon salt*
	1 can (8 ounces) tomatoes; or 1 cup chopped fresh tomatoes
1 cup brown lentils	

Heat oil in a heavy 2-quart pot. Stir in onion and pepper and cook over medium heat for 2 to 3 minutes without browning. Add lentils and stir until hot, 2 to 3 minutes longer. Add water, oregano and salt. Bring to a boil, then lower heat and cook, covered, just until lentils are tender, about 30 minutes. Stir in tomatoes and heat with the lentils for about 5 minutes. Makes 3 cups.

MUSHROOM RAGOUT

1 pound mushrooms	*1/4 cup chopped parsley*
2 tablespoons butter	*1/4 teaspoon salt*
1/2 cup light cream or chicken broth	*A good grating of pepper*

Wipe mushroom caps with a damp cloth and trim a sliver off each stem. Pluck out stems and put as many caps with them to make about half the total volume; chop finely. Cut remaining mushroom caps, if large, into halves or quarters; set aside. Melt butter in a heavy pot or skillet. Stir in chopped mushrooms and cook over medium high heat about 5 minutes. Stir in cream (or broth), about 3/4 of the parsley, salt, pepper and the reserved mushroom caps. Simmer, uncovered, over medium heat for 10 to 15 minutes. Makes about 1 1/2 cups. Serves 4 to 6. Serve with chicken or a salty ham.

CREAMED POTATOES

Potatoes are most delicious and nutritious when steamed or baked with their skins on. (Baked without that horrible wrapping of foil). But here's a simple way to make creamed potatoes.

1 pound potatoes, peeled	*1/2-inch bay leaf, or a few parsley*
1/2 cup water	*stems for flavoring,*
3/4 cup milk	*if you wish*
3/4 teaspoon salt	*2 tablespoons chopped parsley (optional)*

Cut potatoes into tiny dice, 1/4-inch square or smaller. You should have about 2 1/2 cups. Bring water and milk to a simmer in a deep pot about 6 inches in diameter. Stir in potatoes, salt, and bay leaf or parsley stems if used. Simmer, covered, until potatoes are tender, about 20 minutes. Most of liquid will be absorbed; uncover and simmer a few minutes longer if it is not. Sprinkle with parsley and serve. Makes about 2 1/2 cups.

RUTABAGA-POTATO PURÉE

For a very mild flavor use equal quantities potato and rutabaga.

1 pound rutabaga,
peeled and cut in
1/2-inch chunks,
about 3 1/2 cups
1/2 pound potatoes, cut
in 1/2-inch chunks,
about 2 cups

1 tablespoon butter
1 teapoon salt
Black pepper

Put rutabaga chunks in a steamer basket over 1/2 inch of boiling water in a pan. Cover pan and cook 15 minutes. Add potatoes, cover, and continue cooking until both vegetables are tender, about 10 minutes longer. Put vegetables through a food mill set over a heavy pot. Add butter, salt, and black pepper to taste. Stir over heat until hot. Makes 2 1/2 cups. Delicious with pork, beef, duck or goose.

RUTABAGA PANCAKES

Good also made with turnip or daikon radish.

1 egg	*coarsely grated*
2 *tablespoons milk,*	*peeled rutabaga*
yogurt or sour	*(alias yellow turnip)*
cream	*1/4 cup finely chopped*
1/2 teaspoon salt	*scallions or onion*
A little black pepper	*Oil or butter*
2 *cups (1/2 pound)*	

In a small bowl, whisk together the egg, milk, salt and pepper. Stir in grated rutabaga and onion. Heat a heavy iron skillet and grease lightly with oil or butter. Make four pancakes, each with a quarter cupful of the mixture: put mixture into griddle and press down with a spatula. When brown on bottom, turn over and brown on second side, again pressing pancakes with the spatula. When brown, remove to a baking dish. Make another four pancakes with remaining mixture. Put baking dish into a 350° F. oven and let pancakes finish cooking for 8 to 10 minutes. Makes 8 pancakes. Good with duck or pork.

ACORN AND BUTTERNUT SQUASH

You can steam these whole, then cut in half and remove seeds. Serve with butter, salt, and pepper. Or cut squash in half, scoop out seeds and put 1/2 teaspoon butter and a little salt and pepper in each half. Cover tightly with foil. Set in a pan with 1/2 inch of water in it and bake for about 40 minutes at 350° F.

SWEET POTATOES AND YAMS

I love pale-fleshed sweet potatoes simply steamed, or baked at 350° F. for about 40 minutes, and served with butter, salt and pepper. Here's a good way to cook either yams or sweet potatoes in a shorter time.

1 pound sweet	*1/2 cup water*
potatoes, peeled	*1 tablespoon soy sauce*
1 tablespoon oil	*1 teaspoon cornstarch*

Cut sweet potatoes into 1/2-inch cubes; you will have about 4 cups. Heat oil in a heavy pot or skillet, add sweet potatoes (they should cover bottom in a single layer) and stir over medium high heat for about 2 minutes. Add all but about 2 tablespoons of the water, cover, and simmer over medium heat until tender, about 10 minutes. Mix rest of water with soy sauce and cornstarch. Mix into sweet potatoes and simmer for a few seconds. Makes about 2 1/2 cups.

TOMATOES, CORN, AND PEPPERS

2 sweet red or green	*1/2 cup finely chopped*
peppers (1/2	*celery*
pound)	*3 to 4 tomatoes (about*
1 tablespoon butter	*3/4 pound)*
1 tablespoon oil	*3 ears of corn*
2 medium onions (6 to	*1 teaspoon salt*
8 ounces) sliced	*Black pepper*
1/8-inch thick	

Halve peppers, discard seeds and stems, and cut into 1/2-inch squares. Heat butter and oil in a heavy pot; stir in peppers, onions and celery. Cook, covered, over medium heat for 10 minutes. Meanwhile, add tomatoes to a pan of boiling water and count slowly to 10; drain immediately and fill pan with cold water to stop tomatoes cooking. Peel off skins, then cut tomatoes in eighths. Cut kernels off corn, then scrape cobs with a knife (or coarse grater) to remove milky part. Mix tomatoes, corn, salt and pepper into onion mixture. Cook, covered, over low heat for 10 minutes. Vegetables will make their own liquid, but check once or twice to make sure. Makes 4 cups. Delicious with broiled chicken or roast pork.

TURNIPS WITH SOUR CREAM AND HORSERADISH

1 pound (3 medium) turnips	*1 teaspoon salt*
1 cup sour cream	*Black pepper*
2 teaspoons prepared horseradish	

Put unpeeled turnips in a steamer basket over 1 inch boiling water in a pan. Cook, covered, until turnips are tender, about 20 minutes. As soon as turnips are cool enough to handle, peel off skins and cut into 1/4-inch slices. Mix sour cream with horseradish, salt and a good grating of pepper. Layer sour cream with turnip slices in a baking dish, beginning with turnips and ending with sour cream. Bake at 350° F. for 10 to 15 minutes until warmed through. Serves 3 to 4. Turnips can be steamed ahead, then peeled and sliced close to finishing time.

DILLED ZUCCHINI

1 pound zucchini	*2 teaspoons dried dillweed*
1 tablespoon butter or oil	*1/4 cup water*
2 tablespoons chopped fresh or	*About 1/2 teaspoon salt*

Trim ends off zucchini, cut into 1/4- to 1/2-inch slices. Heat oil or butter in a heavy pot. Add zucchini and dill and stir over medium heat for 1 minute. Add water, cover pot and cook over medium high heat for about 8 minutes. Gently stir in salt, cover, and cook 2 minutes longer. Makes about 3 cups.

‡ ZUCCHINI, TOMATOES, AND MUSHROOMS

3/4 pound (about 2)
ripe tomatoes
2 ounces (about 5)
mushrooms
3/4 pound zucchini (3
small)

Pinch each of basil,
thyme, and oregano
1/2 teaspoon salt
Black pepper

Cut tomatoes into 1/2-inch chunks and put in a small heavy pot about 6 inches in diameter. Set pot over a medium heat so tomatoes start to cook. Wipe mushrooms, trim a thin slice off each stem, then slice thinly. Scatter over tomatoes. Trim zucchini and cut in 1/4-inch slices; add to pot. Sprinkle with herbs (be stingy rather than generous). By now the tomatoes should be liquid and simmering. Cover pot and let cook over medium low heat until zucchini is tender, about 10 minutes. Gently stir in salt and a little pepper. Makes about 2 1/2 cups. Good with plain broiled meat. (If you're cutting up vegetables from garden, the quantities raw are about: 2 1/2 cups chopped tomatoes, 3/4 cup sliced mushrooms, 2 cups sliced zucchini.)

6

Toss a Fine Salad

A salad brings to the menu vitamins, minerals and necessary roughage deliciously ensconced in the juicy cells of vegetables like lettuce, watercress, cabbage, celery and tomatoes. A salad at least once a day, made carefully by you at home, is a healthy custom. Sometimes the "salad" may just be fresh sliced carrot or green pepper strips, served with a sandwich.

Some pointers for the salad maker:

1. The way ingredients are handled between the field and the table can make a vast difference to the quantity of nutrients you finally eat.

2. You get the most value from salad greens if you grow your own (without toxic sprays), pick them in the cool of the morning or evening and keep them chilled until serving time.

3. In the market, buy only the freshest looking vegetables and greens. Try to go to market in a flexible frame of mind so that you can switch your menu plans if the vegetables you had set your mind on just don't measure up. The longer the time elapsed between picking and eating, in most cases, the greater the loss of vitamins and minerals. Tomatoes can continue to ripen after picking, and avocados do. Beware of lettuce that has obviously had several tiers of leaves plucked off—it has been around much

too long. When there's a choice between carrots and radishes in plastic bags or with their tips still on, choose the ones with the fresh greens because you know it's not too long since they left the ground, and trim off the tops as soon as you get home.

Probably the worst bargains in nutrition are the plastic packages of pre-cut so-called tossed salad or coleslaw.

4. Over a period of time serve a wide variety of salad greens such as romaine, endive, chicory, Belgian endive, Bibb and Boston lettuce. Use watercress, arugala (also called rocket or roquette), young beet or radish leaves, dandelion leaves, and regular or New-Zealand-type spinach.

5. Be sure to use all the dark green outside leaves (unless brown or damaged), as they contain more vitamins than pale leaves. For that reason, choose dark salad greens more often than pale iceberg lettuce or Belgian endive. If outside leaves are tough, shred them finely before adding to the salad, or make a chiffonade salad entirely of shredded leaves.

6. Wash salad greens quickly in cold water. If you soak them for long, some of the water-soluble nutrients will leach out—and go down the drain with the water. I don't think there's any need to wash the tightly packed inside leaves of cabbage and head lettuce unless soil is visible, but the United Fresh Fruit and Vegetable Association recommends that you do wash them.

7. Put washed leaves in a wire salad basket to drain, or in a good-sized piece of cheesecloth which you can use over and over again. Whichever you use, take it into the backyard, garage or basement; apartment dwellers can stand outside the bathtub holding the basket of lettuce inside drawn curtains. Hold tightly onto the basket or cheesecloth and "throw" it hard. Keep doing this until when you "throw" the basket no more water shakes out. With every few "throws," shake the basket gently to loosen the lettuce.

This is the easiest and fastest way to remove water from lettuce and a task children adore since they can aim the water at each other. If leaves are still wet, pat dry with cloth or paper towel.

8. Chill washed greens unless serving them immediately. Put in refrigerator vegetable drawer or in plastic bags to prevent dehydration and wilting.

9. Cut or tear leaves into pieces as close to serving time as

possible to minimize vitamin loss. For the same reason, don't leave cut greens exposed to light and air longer than necessary. You don't have to turn into a fanatic about all this, but often it's just as easy to do things the better way.

10. Put the leaves into a salad bowl. Use a wooden, glass, china or properly-glazed pottery bowl. (I prefer something like a stoneware bowl or an old tureen which compliments the greens and can be thoroughly washed after each salad.)

Pour oil over the greens then toss with a pair of salad servers until shiny all over. You can do this ten minutes or so before serving.

At the table, or in the kitchen just before serving, add vinegar, salt and seasonings and toss greens again. These ingredients cause lettuce to wilt and so are added only at the last minute.

11. Use a variety of oils for salad making. Buy soy oil one time, perhaps sunflower, safflower or corn oil the next. Buy oils free from additives or preservatives and once opened, store in refrigerator. Use olive oil for flavor, alone or combined with other oil. "Cold-pressed" oils, owing to the heat involved in processing are probably very little different nutritionally from regular oils, but there is a wide variety of flavors available. "Crude" oils, sometimes available in health food stores, do contain more nutrients. Because of the small demand they are expensive. Each kind has it's own pronounced flavor, which may take getting used to. To dilute a strong flavor, mix crude oil with a tasteless refined soy or corn oil.

12. Salad dressings made at home with vegetable oils can be made a modest source of desirable unsaturated fatty acids. If you're trying to cut calories, cut *down* on the amount of dressing used, but don't cut it out altogether unless you are including vegetable oils elsewhere in the menu.

13. Different vinegars can vary salads. Rice vinegar, available in Oriental groceries, is my favorite and worth seeking out. Otherwise, cider vinegar makes the best all-round vinegar. Keep red wine vinegar on hand if you like, and tarragon vinegar too. Distilled white vinegar is too strong for salads. If you prefer, lemon juice may almost always be used instead of vinegar.

14. A salad of tossed greens may be the most popular but try to serve other kinds of salad often. Almost every vegetable, raw

or cooked, can make a delicious salad. An appetizer salad can sneak extra vegetables into a menu, combined perhaps with cheese, meat, fish or egg for protein. For a family, a large salad served informally in the kitchen before dinner can appease impatient young appetitites in a healthy way.

15. In almost every recipe the yield is given in cups in the hope that this will make portion figuring easier.

Menu-Maker's Guide

Crunchy salads to serve as a first course, or with a main course:

‡ Tossed Green Salad
‡ Mustard Cauliflower Salad
  Cabbage, Celery and Radish Salad
  Cabbage, Cucumber and Avocado Salad
  Carrot-Orange Salad
  Greek Salad with Feta Cheese and Olives

Salads which taste better by themselves as appetizers:

‡ Pear, Melon and Cucumber Salad
‡ Green Pepper-Cheese Salad
  Eggplant-Mushroom Salad
  Smashed Radishes
  Melon Curry Salad
  Alfalfa-Pineapple Salad

A cereal salad, to serve with a main course, or as an appetizer:

‡ Bulgur-Mint Salad (Tabbouleh)

Salads to boost the protein in a meal, or to be a main part of a vegetarian meal:

‡ Red Lentil Salad
  Lentils (or Beans) Vinaigrette

Salads to serve with a main course, but in smaller quantities than the crunchy salad category because you can't eat too much of them:

‡ Roast Peppers
  Caraway Beet Salad
  Dilled Cucumbers

Eggplant-Mushroom Salad
Sliced Cucumbers with Green Pepper Dressing
Alfalfa Sprout and Raw Mushroom Salad

Cooked Marinated Vegetables:

Zucchini Salad
Hot Carrot Salad

Two rather high-calorie lunch salads:

Spinach, Bacon, Avocado and Pumpkin Seed Salad
Greek Salad

‡ TOSSED GREEN SALAD

THE GREENS

Some salad makers like to combine as many different greens as possible, but that can make for "confusion" salad. Better to combine just two, three or even four ingredients and let their flavors and textures stand out. But it depends; if you have a garden with a variety of greens growing, you might want to pick some of every kind all at once for a salad. On the other hand, two people with a small refrigerator are better off buying just one or two kinds of greens at a time and using them up quickly.

For the basic greens choose from romaine, endive, chicory, oak leaf lettuce, and the curly lettuce called "salad bowl." Use watercress, arugala, Belgian endive and alfalfa sprouts. In small amounts, use spinach leaves, young beet, radish or turnip tops.

A good salad can be made from any of the above. For decoration, interest, and flavor variety you might sometimes add sliced raw mushrooms, trimmed radishes, trimmed or sliced green onions, slices of avocado, celery or zucchini, thin slices of red or sweet onion. Quartered tomatoes can be good, but they are best when sliced and made into a salad by themselves with oil and vinegar dressing.

Cabbage tastes good as a basic green, alone or combined with watercress. Cabbage doesn't combine very well with lettuce; it tends to overshadow the taste and texture of that more tender green. Chinese cabbage makes an excellent green, alone or with endive.

On occasion you might want to add sliced white radish, thin sticks of carrot, turnip or kohlrabi, tiny cauliflower flowerets, thin strips of green or red peppers, thin sticks of celery, or sliced zucchini.

THE DRESSING

The most delicious, adaptable and widely used dressing is made of oil, vinegar and seasonings. Tastes vary but 3 parts oil to one part vinegar produces a flavor that's neither too oily nor too vinegary. It's up to you; many people prefer four parts oil to one of vinegar. And seasonings such as French mustard add a vinegary taste of their own. If using garlic, prepare it this way for freshest flavor: chop and leave on a board. Sprinkle with salt, then mash quickly with the blade of a chopping knife until creamy. This way you get a marvelous fresh taste but no one chomps down on a chunk of garlic.

Chopped fresh herbs are delicious in salad. Use parsley and chives with abandon, strong herbs like basil, mint, chervil, dill, savory, tarragon and thyme with discretion. Rosemary and bay don't complement salad greens. Omit herbs from salad if used heavily elsewhere in the same meal.

THE MAKING

Put the prepared greens in the salad bowl. (How much is up to you, and what's for dinner.) Break leaves into small pieces if you wish, but try and leave them as large as possible even if you do have to pick up a small romaine leaf or whole stalk of watercress with your fingers to eat. Leaves are beautiful, indistinguishable shreds are not.

Add the oil to the bowl, about 3 tablespoons for four persons (less if you're calorie counting). Using salad servers, toss greens until shiny and coated with oil; push to one side. In bottom of bowl put (to 3 tablespoons oil) 1 tablespoon vinegar, 1/2 teaspoon salt, garlic and French mustard if used, and a good grating of black pepper. Mix together, then toss with the greens just before serving.

‡ MUSTARD CAULIFLOWER SALAD

Either make the dressing ahead, chill it, and add the chilled, freshly cut-up vegetables just before serving, or make salad completely and chill thirty minutes or longer before serving.

Cooked peeled shrimp are delicious added to this salad.

MUSTARD DRESSING

2 *eggs*
1/2 *cup mayonnaise*
1/2 *teaspoon salt*
2 *tablespoons lemon juice*

5 *teaspoons Dijon-style mustard*

VEGETABLES

1 *small head cauliflower (about 1 pound)*
1/2 *cup shredded carrot*
1 *cup thinly sliced celery*

1 *cup thinly sliced radishes, red or white*
1/2 *cup finely sliced green onions*

Take eggs from refrigerator and put into a small pan. Cover with cold water and bring to boil over medium heat. Simmer slowly 10 minutes. Put the hard-cooked eggs in cold water for a minute or two to stop further cooking, then remove shells and chop. Put into a mixing or serving bowl. Mix with mayonnaise, salt, lemon juice and mustard. Chill if you wish. Cut heavy stem and tough outer leaves from cauliflower. With a knife, slice the cauliflower finely; it will fall into smallish pieces. Grate the thickest part of the stem on a coarse grater. You should have about 3 cups cut up cauliflower. Mix it at once with the dressing. Prepare the other vegetables and mix each with the dressing as soon as possible. Serve salad right away, or chill for thirty minutes. Makes 6 cups. Can be served as a first course or accompaniment.

CABBAGE, CELERY, AND RADISH SALAD

The low-calorie yogurt dressing brings out the true flavor of cabbage, which is often lost under thick mayonnaise dressing.

1/2 cup yogurt
1/2 teaspoon salt
2 teaspoons olive oil
Freshly ground
black pepper
3/4 cup sliced red or
white radishes

1 1/2 cups thinly sliced
celery
3 cups shredded
cabbage (a good
1/2 pound)

In salad bowl, mix yogurt with salt, olive oil and pepper. Prepare and add vegetables. Mix gently. Makes 4 cups, serves 4.

CARROT-ORANGE SALAD

Here's a way to serve citrus fruit at dinner instead of breakfast.

1/4 cup orange juice
1/4 cup lemon juice
1 teaspoon salt
2 drops Tabasco
sauce; or a tiny
pinch of crushed hot
red pepper
1/8 teaspoon finely
minced or grated
fresh gingerroot

2 oranges
2 cups coarsely grated
carrots
1/4 cup seedless raisins
(optional)

Put orange juice, lemon juice, salt, Tabasco sauce and gingerroot in a bowl. Using a serrated knife and a sawing motion, remove peel and pith together from each orange. Now hold a peeled orange in one hand and cut down one side of the white membrane that separates each segment; as you approach the center of the orange turn the knife and scoop out the segment into the bowl. Repeat until all segments are removed and just a bundle of membrane remains in your hand. Squeeze membrane over bowl to extract any remaining juice. Add carrots to orange segments and mix gently. Chill for 30 minutes or longer. Meanwhile soak raisins in 1/4 cup warm water to plump them. Drain off any remaining water. Add to carrots and oranges just before serving. Makes about 2 1/2 cups. If you wish, peel and thinly slice an avocado. Put about 3 slices in the bottom of each individual serving bowl, then spoon the orange-carrot mixture over.

CABBAGE, CUCUMBER AND AVOCADO SALAD

1/4 cup oil
2 cups shredded cabbage (about 6 ounces)
1 cucumber, peeled and thinly sliced
1 green pepper, seeds removed, cut in very thin strips
6 radishes, thinly sliced

2 tablespoons finely sliced scallions (optional)
1 avocado
2 tablespoons lime juice
2 tablespoons cider vinegar
1/2 teaspoon salt
Black pepper

Put the oil in a serving bowl, add cabbage and toss lightly. Add cucumber, green pepper, radishes and scallions; toss again. Peel avocado, cut in half and remove pit. Cut into thin narrow strips. Add with lime juice, cider vinegar, salt and a good grating of black pepper to bowl. Toss all together and serve. Makes about 4 cups.

GREEK SALAD WITH FETA CHEESE AND OLIVES

1 teaspoon salt	*1/2 to 1 cucumber,*
1/2 teaspoon crumbled	*peeled*
dried mint leaves;	*1 to 2 tomatoes,*
or 2 tablespoons	*quartered*
chopped fresh mint	*Sweet red or white*
1 tablespoon lemon	*onion (optional)*
juice	*10 or more black*
1 small romaine	*olives, preferably*
lettuce (about 1/2	*Greek*
pound, or 6 cups	*4 ounces Feta cheese,*
torn up)	*broken into small*
3 tablespoons oil,	*pieces*
preferably olive	

Put salt, mint and lemon juice in a small bowl; leave. Have lettuce washed, drained, chilled and torn into serving pieces. Toss lettuce with oil in serving bowl. Cut cucumber in 6 slices lengthwise and then in 1-inch chunks. Arrange on top of lettuce with tomatoes, several thin slices sweet onion, the olives and Feta cheese. At the table just before serving, stir up the mint, lemon juice and salt, sprinkle over the salad and toss well. Makes about 7 cups.

‡ PEAR, MELON AND CUCUMBER SALAD

A cool and refreshing salad for a hot day and best served as a course by itself. It's great for a picinic, and holds up well for at least a day, so don't worry about leftovers.

1 1/2 cups honeydew	*5 tablespoons oil*
melon chunks (about	*2 tablespoons vinegar*
1/3 melon)	*1/4 teaspoon salt*
1 1/2 cups cucumber	*1 sliced scallion or 1*
chunks (2 small	*teaspoon minced*
cucumbers)	*chives*
1 1/2 cups thin sliced	*Fresh black pepper*
pears (2 Bartlett or	
Anjou pears)	

Try to have the fruit chilled and, before you cut it up, make the dressing: Mix oil, vinegar, salt, scallion and a good grating of pepper in a serving bowl. Use a stainless knife to cut up the fruit: Peel rind off melon, cut into smallish bite-size chunks. Mix gently with dressing. Peel cucumber, cut into similar-sized chunks and mix with dressing. Peel the pears or not, cut in quarters, remove core and slice thinly; mix with dressing. Salad can be served right away or chilled for 1 hour. Makes about 4 1/2 cups. Instead of pears you can use 1 1/2 cups finely sliced green pepper.

‡ GREEN PEPPER-CHEESE SALAD

This salad makes a perfectly lovely appetizer. The trick is in cutting the pieces small so the total result is an interesting texture as well as good combination of flavors.

3/4 pound green peppers, preferably the pale green Italian "fryers"	3 tablespoons oil
	1 tablespoon cider vinegar
	1/4 teaspoon salt
8 ounces Swiss cheese, preferably Switzerland Swiss	1 teaspoon Dijon-style mustard

Remove the seeds and stem from the peppers and cut them into fine julienne shreds—roughly the size of a kitchen match. Cut the cheese into similar size strips. Wrap and chill until serving time. For the dressing, mix the remaining ingredients in serving bowl. Just before serving add the cheese and peppers and toss together. Makes 3 cups, serves 4 as an appetizer.

Children may prefer a dressing of 1/2 cup mayonnaise with 2 tablespoons water mixed in to thin it down. Season with 1 teaspoon Dijon-style mustard.

EGGPLANT-MUSHROOM SALAD

*1 eggplant, weighing
  about 1 1/2 pounds*
*1/4 cup finely chopped
  onion*
2 tablespoons oil
*1/2 cup chopped
  mushrooms*

*1 teaspoon chopped
  garlic (optional)*
1 teaspoon salt
*1/4 cup chopped parsley
  (optional)*

Wash the eggplant and put in oven on middle shelf. Bake for 15 minutes at 500° F. Insert a wooden or metal skewer, and if the center still seems raw and hard, bake eggplant about 5 minutes longer. Cool for a few minutes. Sauté onion in oil until translucent, about 1 minute. Add mushrooms and stir over medium heat until lightly browned, about 1 minute longer. Remove from heat. Discard stem of eggplant; chop skin and pulp coarsely. Mix with mushrooms and onions. On a board with the blade of a knife, crush garlic with salt to a smooth paste. Mix into eggplant along with parsley. Chill. Makes 2 cups. Serve as an appetizer or relish.

Here's another interesting way to serve this salad: Slice ripe tomatoes, douse them with oil, vinegar, seasonings and herbs, let marinate 2 to 3 hours. At serving time, heap eggplant salad in the middle of a platter, and surround with the tomato salad.

SMASHED RADISHES

Radishes, surprisingly perhaps, contain worthwhile amounts of calcium, niacin, and vitamin C.

1 bunch radishes
1/4 teaspoon salt
1 teaspoon soy sauce
*1 tablespoon cider
  vinegar*

1 tablespoon honey
*1 teaspoon oil, sesame
  oil if you have it.*

Trim "tails" off radishes, and cut off leaves leaving 1/2 inch of the green for decoration. Discard any wilted leaves, wash remaining ones and drain well. Wash and drain radishes. Mix remaining ingredients in a bowl. Using a wooden pestle, bottom of a bottle, or the heel of your hand, "smash" each radish. Don't take out all your aggressions and smash the radishes to pieces, just crack them open. Mix radishes with dressing; this can be done 10 to 15 minutes before serving. Seconds before serving, cut radish leaves into 1/2-inch strips and mix with radishes and dressing. Serve as a relish. Makes 1 cup.

MELON CURRY SALAD

The curry dressing can be prepared several hours ahead and chilled.

1 teaspoon curry powder	*1/3 cup heavy cream*
1 tablespoon lemon juice	*3 cups small cubes of cantaloupe or watermelon*
1 tablespoon cider vinegar	*Lettuce leaves*

Mix curry powder, lemon juice and cider vinegar in a small bowl. Let stand 5 minutes. Whip cream until thick but not really stiff. Stir curry mixture gently into the whipped cream, then carefully mix in the melon cubes. Chill 10 minutes. Serve spooned into individual lettuce leaves. Makes 3 cups, serves about 6 as an appetizer.

ALFALFA-PINEAPPLE SALAD

3 tablespoons oil	*1 can (20 ounces) pineapple chunks packed in pineapple juice; or 2 cups chunked fresh pineapple*
1 tablespoon rice or cider vinegar	
1/4 teaspoon salt	
Black pepper	
4 to 5 cups alfalfa sprouts (page 174)	

Put the oil, vinegar, salt and a good grating of black pepper in serving bowl. Gently mix in alfalfa sprouts. Drain pineapple thoroughly. Add to alfalfa sprouts and toss again. Makes about 4 1/2 cups salad.

‡ BULGUR-MINT SALAD (TABBOULEH)

This salad is best chilled—but in an emergency it's quite delicious served right away. Often romaine leaves are stuck into the top of the salad; to eat, you scoop up a mouthful on a leaf.

1/2 cup coarse, fine or medium bulgur	*1 1/2 teaspoons salt*
1/2 cup boiling water	*1 teaspoon crushed dried mint; or*
1 cup loosely packed parsley sprigs	*1 to 2 tablespoons chopped fresh mint*
1/4 cup red onion, cut into chunks (optional)	*1/4 cup olive oil*
	About 4 tablespoons lemon juice

Put bulgur in a bowl and add boiling water. Let stand 10 minutes, then stir gently. Water will have been absorbed into bulgur. Now put remaining ingredients, with just 3 tablespoons of lemon juice, into an electric blender and whir. You'll get a creamy dressing with green flecks in it. Taste, add remaining tablespoon of lemon juice if you wish. Mix dressing with bulgur. Chill well. Makes 1 1/2 cups salad. Serve as appetizer, salad or buffet dish.

If you don't have a blender, chop onion and parsley very, very fine, then mix with other ingredients.

‡ RED LENTIL SALAD

This is delicious and can be served as main course, appetizer or salad. It keeps very well, so make double or triple quantity and have extra on hand. For best nutrition include a little meat, milk, fish or cheese in the meal.

1 cup red lentils	*1 teaspoon salt*
2 cups cold water	*2 1/2 tablespoons red*
2 strips bacon	*wine vinegar*
1/4 cup thinly sliced	*Black pepper*
scallions or finely	
chopped onion	

Put lentils in a strainer and rinse quickly with cold water. Put in a heavy pot with 2 cups of cold water. Bring to a simmer then cook, covered, for 30 minutes. Stir once or twice. Lentils will become a pale purée. Meanwhile, cook bacon in a skillet until crisp. Remove and drain well. Pour off all but about 1 tablespoon of the fat. When lentils are cooked, add scallions to hot bacon fat in skillet and sauté a few minutes without browning. Add salt and wine vinegar, then stir in lentils and bacon broken into small pieces. Season with black pepper. Serve warm, hot or cold. Makes 2 cups.

Brown Lentil Salad: Make as for red lentil salad using 1 cup brown lentils, 2 cups water. Simmer for 20 minutes only; lentils will stay whole. Add 1/2 cup diced celery, 1/2 teaspoon salt to the pot for last 5 minutes of cooking. Use only 1/2 teaspoon salt in dressing.

LENTILS VINAIGRETTE

4 cups water	*1 tablespoon capers,*
1 cup brown lentils	*rinsed and drained*
3 tablespoons oil	*2 tablespoons finely*
1 tablespoon cider	*chopped dill pickle*
vinegar	*2 tablespoons finely*
1 tablespoon finely	*chopped parsley*
sliced chives or	*1/2 teaspoon salt*
scallions	

Bring water to boil in a 2-to-3-quart pot. Pour in lentils. Simmer, covered, for 15 to 20 minutes. When done, lentils should be tender but not broken up. Drain off any water. Put remaining ingredients in a serving bowl. Mix with a wooden spoon. Add warm lentils to bowl and mix gently. Serve right away or chill. Makes 3 cups.

‡ ROAST PEPPERS

In the Middle East where this salad comes from, the peppers are impaled on a stick or fork and roasted over an open flame or charcoal. If you have a gas range, you can broil peppers directly over the flame. Roast peppers keep well for several days, so make plenty when you have a glut.

1 pound sweet red or green peppers (about 4 medium)	*1/2 teaspoon salt*
	Black pepper
	2 tablespoons olive oil

Put peppers under the broiler as close to heat as possible. Broil until skins blister and char in patches. Use tongs to turn. When blistered all over (this only takes 5 to 10 minutes) let peppers cool a few minutes until you can rub and peel off the skins. Cut peeled peppers open, letting any juice fall into serving bowl. Discard seeds and stems; cut peppers into strips about 1/2-inch wide. Put in serving bowl and mix with salt, black pepper and oil. Serve chilled or at room temperature. Makes 2 cups. Delicious alone, or mixed with sliced tomatoes.

Roast Peppers with Hot Garlic Dressing: Crush 1 teaspoon chopped garlic with 3/4 teaspoon salt. Melt 1 tablespoon butter in a pan. Add the garlic, mix around, then add the peppers. Stir over medium heat until peppers are warm; sprinkle with black pepper and serve.

CARAWAY BEET SALAD

1 bunch beets (about 1 1/2 pounds)	*1/4 cup boiling water*
	1/4 cup vinegar
2 teaspoons caraway seeds	*2 tablespoons honey*

Trim tops off beets, leaving an inch of stalk. Wash beets. Put in a steamer basket over 1 inch of boiling water in a pan. Cover pan and cook over medium heat until beets are tender, 20 to 30 minutes, or longer, depending on size. Let cool. Meanwhile, crush caraway seeds in a bowl with the end of a rolling pin (or use a mortar and pestle). Pour boiling water over seeds. Let stand 5 to 10 minutes. Mix in vinegar and honey. Rub skins off beets with your hands. Cut beets into thin slices, dice or julienne strips. Mix with dressing and let marinate for at least an hour before serving. Makes about 3 cups.

DILLED CUCUMBERS

Home grown or unwaxed cucumbers need not be peeled. Thin slices of sweet onion can be mixed with the cucumber.

1/2 cup sour cream	*3/4 teaspoon salt*
1/2 cup yogurt	*2 cucumbers*
1 teaspoon dried dillweed or 1 tablespoon snipped fresh dill	

Mix sour cream, yogurt, dill and salt in serving bowl. Peel chilled cucumbers. Slice thinly. Mix with dressing. Serve at once, or cover and chill for thirty minutes. Makes about 3 cups.

SLICED CUCUMBERS WITH GREEN PEPPER DRESSING

Cucumbers are not well endowed with vitamins A or C; the green pepper dressing adds a small boost in that direction.

1/3 cup diced green pepper	*1 teaspoon dried dillweed or 1 tablespoon snipped fresh dill (optional)*
1/3 cup yogurt	
1/3 cup sour cream	*2 cucumbers*
1/4 teaspoon salt	

Put green pepper in electric blender with about half the yogurt. Whir until pale, green and creamy looking. You may need to stop blender once and push everything down. Mix gently with remaining yogurt, sour cream, salt and dill (if used) in serving bowl. Chill, or use at once. Peel chilled cucumbers. Slice thinly with stainless knife. Mix gently with dressing. Makes about 3 cups.

ALFALFA SPROUT AND RAW MUSHROOM SALAD

If you wish, make double the dressing and add 2 to 3 cups broken up romaine leaves to the salad. Avocado slices taste good with sprouts too; if used, omit mushrooms.

1/4 teaspoon minced garlic	Black pepper
3/4 teaspoon salt	About 1 cup thinly sliced fresh mushrooms
3 tablespoons oil	3 cups alfalfa sprouts
3 teaspoons vinegar	

On a board with the blade of a knife, crush garlic with salt to a smooth paste. Put in serving bowl. Mix in oil, vinegar, and a good grating of black pepper. Add mushrooms and toss with dressing; this can be done 10 to 15 minutes before serving. Add alfalfa sprouts and toss again. Makes about 3 1/2 cups.

MARINATED VEGETABLES

There are people whose insides simply cannot cope with hard vegetables such as cauliflower, carrots or cabbage when served in the raw. A cooked vegetable salad is delicious and solves the problem.

ZUCCHINI SALAD

1 pound zucchini or summer squash	*1/2 teaspoon salt*
2 teaspoons cider vinegar	*1/2 teaspoon dried dillweed or 1 tablespoon snipped fresh dill*
2 tablespoons oil	

Wash the squash and put in a steamer basket over 1/2 inch boiling water in a pan. Cover pan and cook over medium heat until tender, but still slightly firm. For squash about 2 inches in diameter this takes approximately 15 minutes. Mix remaining ingredients in serving bowl. As soon as squash is cool enough to handle, trim off the ends. Cut squash in 8 slices lengthwise then in 1-inch strips. Mix lightly with dressing. Serve warm or chilled. Makes 2 cups.

Hot Carrot Salad: Cook 1 pound scrubbed or peeled carrots as above. Cut the same way and mix with same dressing. Serve warm or chilled. Makes about 3 cups. Parsnips are delicious served like this, also green beans and fresh fava beans. These marinated vegetables can be mixed with greens in a tossed salad in which case no other dressing may be needed.

SPINACH, BACON, AVOCADO AND PUMPKIN SEED SALAD

Make this salad with really fresh spinach. The contents of plastic bags of spinach are usually too broken up to be suitable; buy it loose.

Malabar or New Zealand spinach can be used instead of the regular kind, and it is usually fine when packed in a plastic bag.

Slices of Canadian bacon, lightly browned and used instead of regular bacon, will give you more protein, less fat. Use 4 to 6 slices.

1/4 pound fresh spinach (about 4 cups leaves after trimming)	*1 tablespoon vinegar*
6 strips bacon	*1/2 teaspoon salt*
1 cup peeled, cubed, ripe avocado	*1 tablespoon pumpkin kernels*

Trim off tough stems from spinach. Wash leaves well and whirl dry in salad basket or cheesecloth. Chill. Cook bacon until crisp. Drain well and break each strip into four pieces. This much can be done ahead. Put avocado cubes, vinegar and salt in serving bowl. Toss well with two wooden spoons so that the avocado breaks up quite considerably. This will be the "dressing" for the salad. At moment of serving, add spinach leaves to bowl and toss well. Add bacon and pumpkin seeds and toss again. Serves 1 as a main dish for lunch.

7

Desserts Can Be
Good for You

Many of the packaged sweet things in life today are practically free—of any nutritional value. But desserts can be made with fruit, milk, whole grains and eggs to contribute plenty of protein, vitamins and minerals for no more calories than desserts of sugar, shortening and refined grains.

Most packaged convenience desserts consist largely of sugar, or saturated fat in the form of shortening or coconut oil. Fat and sugar together are currently suspected of contributing to heart disease and other medical problems. For this reason, avoid dessert toppings (frozen, or whipped up from a mix), ready-made baked goods and cake mixes. Packaged gelatin desserts contribute no vitamins at all, only a very small amount of low-grade protein and an enormous amount of sugar. Both coloring and flavoring are artificial. If your family loves gelatin desserts, make them yourself, quickly, easily and inexpensively, using fresh, frozen or canned fruit juice, and unflavored gelatin.

Fruit is the foundation of many good desserts and once again the question is whether or not to peel fruit such as apples, pears and peaches. Quite a large proportion of the vitamins lie under the skin and may be discarded if the fruit is peeled. On the other hand, any spray residues may lurk there too. I don't think there's a simple answer. If apples and pears have been coated with wax, it's probably a good idea to peel them. Otherwise, wash the fruit (I use soap and a Japanese vegetable brush) and rinse thoroughly. A few people find that hard fruit skins irritate the throat in which case, of course, the peel should be removed, but as thinly as possible.

In these recipes honey is used instead of sugar. Honey has no magical properties as some people would have you believe, or if it has I've never been lucky enough to notice them! But it may be slightly easier for the body to cope with. I don't think it's necessary to be fanatic about eliminating sugar entirely from the diet. But we do need to reduce our consumption of sugar and when using it to make sure it is in combination with good nutritious ingredients. Honey is "sweeter" than sugar and does contain a tiny sprinkling of nutrients. In adapting your own recipes, should you wish to, 1/4 of a cup of honey can usually replace 1/2 cup of sugar. Sometimes a mixture of half honey, half molasses, not only increases the nutritional value of cookies and cakes, but imparts a delightful new flavor.

Love is not feeding your family or yourself highly concentrated sweets. Love is serving satisfying desserts that go easy on sugar, flour, cream, butter and honey, and strong on ingredients that contribute to their well-being.

Menu-Makers Guide

Fruit Desserts:

>   Fresh Fruit
>   Sour Cream Honey or Yogurt Dip for fruit
>   Ricotta Cheese with Fruit
> ‡ Hattit Kit to serve with fruit
>   Fresh Fruit Compotes
>   Cooked Fruit Compotes
> ‡ Cranberry Kissel
>   Apricot-Orange Mousse
> ‡ Persian Apples
> ‡ Close-to-Nature Applesauce
>   Poached Apples with Raw Oranges

Hard Old Peaches Poached
‡ Plum Fool
‡ Quick Prune-Walnut Pudding
Banana Cottage-Cheese Cream

Desserts Made with Milk, and Grains or Fruit:

‡ Quick Indian Pudding
Oatmeal Molasses Cream
Pumpkin Caramel Custard
Natural Rice Pudding, English Style
Barley Pudding
Brown Barley Pudding
Monday Rice
‡ Apple Rice, using leftover rice
Illegal Ice Cream

Cookies and Cakes:

Yeasted Whole-Wheat Apple Cake
Yogurt Cottage Cheese Cake
Austrian Curd Cake
Cranberry Cinnamon Oat Streusel
Corn Crisp
Wheat Germ, Oatmeal and Raisin Cookies
Whole-Wheat Peanut Squares

Candy:

‡ Chinese Sweet Bean Paste
Date and Walnut Candy
‡ Carrot Halva

Fresh Fruit

The simplest, most delicious, healthful and work-free of desserts is a big bowl of fresh fruit set on the table. Give each person a small plate and a knife and let him dig in. Apples, oranges, pears, bananas and grapes can all be mixed in a bowl. Put softer fruits like berries, peaches, plums, cherries and nectarines in a bowl or on a platter by themselves to avoid bruising. If you have a grapevine, pluck a leaf or two occasionally and put under berries or plums for decoration.

If a meal has been very satisfying, fresh fruit will suffice for dessert. But if there's a gap to fill, serve cheese and bread or crackers with the fruit. Put one or more cheeses on a plate or board and let everyone help himself. If you don't have a fancy cheese store, select cheeses which are available in your supermarket like Cheddar, Muenster, blue, or a pungent, ripe Liederkranz. If you have a good source for cheeses nearby, try a new one now and then such as Taleggio, Brie, Camembert, Havarti, Boursin (without garlic and herbs), Boursault, Crema Dania, Tomme au Marc (with a coating of black grape seeds), Kuminost (with caraway seeds), and so on.

Raisins, and almond or sunflower seeds, are absolutely delicious served with fruit and cheese. Sometime you might like to try the English custom of finishing a meal with fresh celery, cheese and crackers.

SOUR CREAM HONEY DIP FOR FRESH FRUIT

1/2 cup sour cream   *1 teaspoonful honey*

Mix sour cream and honey together in a small bowl. Set on a platter and surround with fresh fruit, cut up or whole. Makes 1/2 cup, serves 2 to 3.

YOGURT HONEY DIP

1/2 cup yogurt   *2 teaspoons honey*

Put about a tablespoonful of the yogurt in a small bowl. Add honey and mix well. Stir in remaining yogurt. Makes 1/2 cup, serves 2 to 3.

RICOTTA CHEESE WITH FRUIT

Ricotta cheese, 3 to 4 ounces per person	*Honey* *Fresh fruit such as grapes, berries, or pears*

Buy ricotta cheese ready-made, from whole or part-skimmed milk. Serve it chilled. Put in a serving bowl or on individual plates. Serve with a spoon or fork, honey to drizzle on top if desired, and fresh fruit.

‡ HATTIT KIT

This delicious curd tastes something like Ricotta cheese. Don't think you can omit heavy cream to cut calories, because if you do you'll get very wet curd tasting almost exactly like yogurt.

2 cups milk *1 cup heavy cream* *2 cups buttermilk*	*Honey and fresh fruit*

Bring milk and cream just to boiling point in a heavy 2–to 3–quart pot. Remove from heat and immediately stir in buttermilk; mixture will curdle. Line a bowl with a double layer of cheesecloth, and have ready about 12 inches of twine. Pour curdled mixture into cheesecloth. Gather up edges and tie with twine. Hang up to drain with bowl underneath to catch the whey that drips out. Leave two hours or longer. Undo cheesecloth, spoon curd into a serving dish. Chill well. At table, everyone spoons some curd onto a plate, adds honey if they wish. Serve with fresh fruit. Makes about 2 1/2 cups, serves 4. Chilled, the whey makes a refreshing drink.

Persimmons are especially delicious with ricotta or Hattit Kit. Use them only when very ripe and squishy soft. To eat, remove green cap and discard. Cut persimmon in halves or quarters. Eat with spoon, scooping tender flesh off tough skins.

Fresh Fruit Compotes

If you'd rather serve fruit to eat from a bowl, with a spoon and perhaps a cookie on the side, then try your hand at fruit compotes. A compote is a single fruit or combination of fruits cut into bite-size pieces and moistened with a sweet liquid. A compote can be made with fresh or dried fruits, cooked or raw. Since it is healthiest to eat a wide variety of foods, a compote is an excellent way to use many kinds of fruits. You can include exotic or expensive fruits without too much cost by mixing them with lower priced and plentiful ones.

The liquid used for compotes can be fruit juice or a syrup of honey and water. Sometimes a very sweet wine is good. If you're going to make compotes often, then it may be simpler to make a bottle or two of honey syrup to keep on hand. You may want to experiment with exotic honeys such as lime blossom, orange blossom, or rosemary. A few drops of orange flower or rose water can be added to a compote; look for these bottled perfumed waters in Middle Eastern stores.

Honey Syrup: Mix 1 cup water with 1/2 cup honey in a bottle. Shake to mix. Store in refrigerator. Use frugally as most fruits will exude some liquid of their own soon after being cut up and mixed in a bowl.

To make a compote put a small amount of honey-syrup into serving bowl, or mix 1/4 cup honey with 1/2 cup water in bowl. Prepare the fruit and mix immediately with the syrup to prevent browning and vitamin loss. Taste juice in bowl; sharpen with lemon juice if you wish. Cover compote and chill until serving time.

Compote Combinations: Cut sweet dessert apples (not sour cookers) peeled or not, in 1/4 to 1/2-inch chunks. Mix with about equal amounts seedless grapes (removed from stems), and fresh orange segments. Or add bananas instead of oranges, close to serving time.

Mixed peeled cubed cantaloupe with halved strawberries, fresh raspberries or red currants. Mix gently so as not to bruise the fruit.

Or, mix any amount or combination of pineapple chunks, melon chunks, grapes, orange or tangerine segments, papaya, peeled sliced kiwi fruit, ripe peaches or nectarines, figs, ripe green or purple plums, blackberries, loganberries, raspberries, strawberries, really ripe apricots, peeled pitted lichees, sweet cherries, blueberries, watermelon or whatever fruit you can find.

Fruits not good in a fresh compote are quince, hard pears, loquats, cranberries, rhubarb, unripe peaches and other unripe stone fruit, or sour cherries. They need to be cooked first.

Cooked Fruit Compotes: Poach cut-up fruit in honey syrup over very low flame just until tender. Sliced peaches, for example, take about 5 minutes. High heat and fast boiling results in broken up, mushy fruit, besides unnecessary vitamin loss. For flavor, strips of lemon rind (cut with a vegetable peeler), cinnamon sticks or cloves may be added to the syrup.

Cooking apples and all the fruits listed as unsuitable for a fresh compote can be poached for a cooked one.

‡ CRANBERRY KISSEL

This is the Russian version of Scandinavian fruit soup. In Russia, kissel often accompanies sweet baked kasha or other cereal as a sauce. Kissel can be made with raspberries, red currants, rhubarb, or even blueberries, though these are better combined with a tarter fruit. It's a good way to use up leftover juice from water-pack canned fruit; sweeten to taste and thicken in the proportion of 1 teaspoon cornstarch to 1 cup liquid.

1 pound (about 5 cups) fresh or frozen cranberries	*2 two-inch strips orange rind, cut with a vegetable peeler (wash first)*
Water	
1 cup honey (part sage honey is delicious)	*Ditto, lemon rind*
	4 teaspoons cornstarch or arrowroot
4 inches cinnamon stick	

Rinse cranberries in a strainer, pick out and discard any squashed or brown ones. Put berries in a stainless or enameled pot with 1 3/4 cups water, the honey, cinnamon stick, orange and lemon rinds. Bring to a boil, then lower heat and let simmer a few minutes until most of the berries have broken up. If you like, fish out a few whole cranberries and put in serving dish for decoration. Mix cornstarch with 1/4 cup cold water. Stir into simmering cranberries and bring to boil. Remove pan from heat and put contents through a strainer or food mill to remove seeds. Mix with whole berries in serving bowl. Serve warm or cold with a crisp cookie, with a spoonful of sour cream or with ice cream. Makes 4 cups.

APRICOT-ORANGE MOUSSE

This is one of the few recipes where egg whites are beaten with any other ingredient without collapsing. If you have no other use for the yolks, drop them whole into a pan of simmering water and let cook over very low heat for 5 minutes. Use in egg salad or push them through a strainer onto a green salad for a golden snow effect.

11 ounces (about 2 1/4 cups) dried apricots*	*1 can (6 ounces) frozen orange juice concentrate, thawed*
2 cups boiling water	*3 egg whites*
1/4 cup honey	

Put apricots in a deep narrow container and pour boiling water over them. Let stand until soft, about 2 hours, or refrigerate for as long as 24 hours. Put apricots, plus any remaining liquid, into an electric blender with honey and thawed concentrate. Blend until smooth. With a rotary beater or electric mixer, whip egg whites until stiff and white. Then gradually beat puréed apricots into egg whites, about 1/2 cup at a time. (By hand, this gets a little hard on the wrists toward the end.) Chill until serving time. Makes about 6 cups. Serve, if you like, topped with whipped cream and slivered toasted almonds.

*Dried apricots are expensive, period, but their delicious flavor makes an occasional splurge worthwhile. Apricots are a good source of vitamin A. When dried, they often have a better flavor than fresh (and as much or more vitamin A) because they are allowed to ripen longer on the tree. Buy unsuphured apricots if you can. Some Middle Eastern stores have them from Turkey. Health food stores may carry very hard, dark ones from California; use 3 cups (about 11 ounces) instead of 2 1/4 cups, and let soak at least 3 hours.

‡ PERSIAN APPLES

In Iran, this dessert is spooned into individual glasses, topped at last moment with a spoonful of crushed ice.

3 tablespoons
lemon juice
2 tablespoons honey

3 to 4 Golden Delicious
apples

Mix lemon juice and honey in serving bowl. Coarsely grate the apples, peeled or unpeeled. Mix lightly with lemon juice and honey. Serve very cold. Makes about 3 cups. Serves 4. Small melon balls can be used instead of apple. Persians sometimes add a few drops of bottled rose water, sold in Middle Eastern stores, to this mixture.

‡ CLOSE-TO-NATURE APPLESAUCE

Applesauce keeps very well in the refrigerator. When apples are plentiful, make a big batch and freeze for winter use.

1 pound green cooking
apples (about 3
medium apples)
1/4 cup honey
3 tablespoons lemon
juice

2 strips lemon rind,
washed then cut
with vegetable
peeler
Pinch ground clove
or cinnamon

Leave apples unpeeled if you can. Quarter and core them, then cut into small pieces. (This recipe is a great way to use up misshapen or wormy apples; measure about 3 cups after cutting up.) Put honey and lemon juice into an electric blender. Add about 1/3 of the cut-up apples and whir smooth. Stop machine and push apples down if necessary. When the purée is whirring nicely, gradually drop in remaining apples. Taste applesauce, add more honey or lemon if you wish. Put into a pot with lemon rind and clove or cinnamon. Bring to a simmer and cook 1 to 2 minutes only. Serve warm or chilled, perhaps with yogurt, cream, or, calories permitting, vanilla ice cream. Makes 2 cups.

Uncooked applesauce is equally delicious. Simply follow above directions until purée is made in blender. Omit lemon rind and spice.

POACHED APPLES WITH RAW ORANGES

Dessert apples, such as Golden Delicious, are best for this dish.

1 cup water	*a vegetable peeler*
3 tablespoons honey	*(wash first)*
2 two-inch strips	*1 pound apples (3*
orange rind, cut	*medium)*
with	*2 to 3 oranges*

Bring water, honey and orange rind to a simmer. Peel apples or not, as you choose; core and cut into eighths. Put enough apple slices in pot with honey-water to make a single layer. Bring to a slow simmer, cover and poach for about 3 minutes. Turn slices over, cover and cook about 4 minutes longer; apple should be just tender and not at all broken up. Lift into a serving bowl with a slotted spoon. Add remaining apple slices to pot and repeat. When finished pour honey-water over apples in bowl. Using a serrated knife and a sawing motion, cut peel and white pith together off oranges. Now, holding oranges over serving bowl one at a time, cut down one side of the white membrane separating each orange segment, and scoop out the segments one by one. Let segments drop into bowl. When you have just a bundle of white membrane left in your hand squeeze it over bowl to extract any juice. Serve dessert chilled or at room temperature. Serves 4 to 6.

For blackberry and apple compote, omit oranges from preceding recipe. After poaching apples add 1 to 2 cups washed blackberries to syrup in pan. Simmer 30 seconds. Mix with apples.

HARD OLD PEACHES POACHED

1 cup water	*1 1/2 pounds (about 5)*
1/2 cup honey	*hard peaches*
1/2 vanilla pod	
(optional)	

Bring water, honey and vanilla pod just to simmering point in a 2- to 3-quart pan. Quickly cut *unpeeled peaches into slices about 1/8-inch thick. You will have about 5 cups of slices. Put all at once into the honey-water. (Don't worry if all are not submerged at first.) Bring just to a simmer, cover pan, and let poach over very low heat for 3 to 5 minutes. When tender, remove peach slices to a serving bowl (or just leave them in the pot if it's good looking). Serve warm or chilled. Makes 3 cups cooked peaches. Leftover peach syrup can be used later to poach more fruit, or it can be used as the syrup in a fresh fruit compote. When peaches are plentiful, poach several batches and freeze for between-season use.

‡ PLUM FOOL

An old, old English dessert that can be made with any tart fruit such as rhubarb or gooseberries. Traditional recipes do not contain cornstarch, but the very short, vitamin-saving cooking time used here produces a wet purée that needs slight thickening.

1 pound green red or	*2 teaspoons cornstarch*
purple plums that	*1 tablespoon water*
are slightly hard	*1/2 cup heavy cream or*
and underripe	*evaporated milk*
2 tablespoons honey	

Cut up and pit plums; do not peel. Put in electric blender and whir until fairly smooth, about 30 seconds. Put into a small pan

---

*If you prefer to peel peaches, drop them into a pan of boiling water and count to 15. Lift out and dip immediately in cold water to stop further cooking. Skins can now be peeled off easily.

with the honey; bring to a simmer and cook for 2 to 3 minutes. Mix cornstarch with water, stir into plum pureé and cook for 1 minute. Remove from heat and let cool. Whip cream or evaporated milk (check can for directions). Gently fold cream into cooled purée. Pour into a serving dish and chill. Makes about 2 2/3 cups, serves 4 or more.

‡ QUICK PRUNE-WALNUT PUDDING

2 eggs
1/4 cup corn or soy oil
1/4 teaspoon salt
1 cup water

1 cup cut-up sour
  prunes, pits
  discarded
1/4 chopped walnuts or
  filberts

To hard-cook eggs, take straight from refrigerator and put into a small pan. Cover with cold water. Bring to boil over medium high heat, then lower heat and let simmer for 12 minutes. Pour off boiling water and add cold to stop further cooking of eggs. Cut each egg in half, right through the shell (quicker than peeling), and scoop contents into an electric blender. Add oil, salt, water and prunes. Turn on machine and blend smooth. Add walnuts, whir briefly to break up. Pour pudding into a serving dish, or individual dishes, and chill well. Serve as is, or topped with more chopped nuts, or toasted wheat germ. Makes about 1 1/2 cups.

BANANA COTTAGE-CHEESE CREAM

2 eggs
2 very ripe bananas*
1 cup pot-style cottage
  cheese

2 tablespoons lemon
  juice
1 tablespoon honey

Bananas are ripe when they have leopardlike skins and are soft to the touch.

To hard-cook eggs, put straight from refrigerator into a small pan. Cover with cold water. Bring to boil over medium heat, then lower heat and let simmer for 12 minutes. Pour off boiling water an add cold to stop further cooking of eggs. Cut each egg in half, right through the shell, and scoop contents into an electric blender. Peel the bananas and add them, too. Whir smooth. Add cottage cheese, lemon juice and honey. Whir again until smooth and fluffy. Pour into a serving dish and chill well. Pudding will firm up while chilling. Makes 2 cups, serves 4.

‡ QUICK INDIAN PUDDING

This old New England dessert is traditionally baked and acquires a lovely skin during the process. The unbaked version, although softer in texture, is often more convenient and very delicious.

4 cups milk	*1/4 teaspoon ground*
1/2 cup stone ground	*ginger*
yellow corn meal	*1/3 cup medium*
1/2 teaspoon salt	*molasses (blackstrap*
1/4 teaspoon ground	*is too strong)*
cinnamon	*2 tablespoons honey*

In heavy 2-quart pan bring milk almost to boil. Pour in corn meal slowly, whisking milk constantly. Add salt. Simmer 10 to 15 minutes over medium heat stirring frequently until thickened. Remove from heat, stir in cinnamon, ginger, molasses and honey. Taste—add more salt, spices or honey if you like. Serve warm or cold. Makes about 4 cups. Serve 4 to 6.

Baked Indian Pudding: Cook pudding as above. Let cool 2 to 3 minutes. Beat in 2 eggs, one at a time. Pour mixture into 1 1/2-quart baking dish. Bake for 35 to 40 minutes at 325° F. Serve warm or cold. Serves 4 to 6.

OATMEAL MOLASSES CREAM

1/4 cup water	*2 tablespoons medium*
1 1/2 tablespoons	*molasses; or 1/4*
freeze-dried coffee*	*cup honey*
(optional)	*2 cups milk*
1 envelope (1	*1/4 cup rolled oats*
tablespoon)	*1/3 cup heavy cream or*
unflavored gelatin	*evaporated milk*
3 egg yolks	

Put water in a small bowl. Stir in coffee, if used, then gelatin. Leave until needed. Whisk egg yolks, molasses and milk in a 2- to 3-quart pot. Put over medium heat and stir constantly. You want eggs to thicken milk slightly but without getting so hot that they curdle. To ensure success, use a thermometer (meat or candy). When it reads between 170° F. and 175° F., custard is as thick as it will get. (If you don't have a thermometer watch for a white foam; about one minute after it disappears the custard is done.) Remove from heat and stir in soaked gelatin. When dissolved, stir in oats. Cool mixture, stirring occasionally until it starts to jell. Whip cream or evaporated milk (see directions on can). Stir one spoonful into custard, then fold in remainder. Pour into a serving dish or 3-cup mold. Chill until firm, about 1 hour. Serve from dish or turn out onto a plate. Makes about 2 3/4 cups.

To reduce cooling period to about 7 minutes: Put lots of ice cubes and a little water in a large bowl, set the pan of custard in it. Stir constantly but slowly until mixture thickens.

CARAMEL SAUCE

2 tablespoons honey	*1 teaspoon cornstarch*
2 tablespoons medium	*1/2 teaspoon lemon*
molasses	*juice*
1/2 cup water	

Put honey and molasses in a 1-quart pan. Cook over medium heat for about 3 minutes. Mixture will bubble, and the bubbles

*If you omit the coffee you may like to serve the following sauce with the dessert.

will get quite large. Immediately pour into pan all but about 2 tablespoons of the water. Stir over medium heat. Mix cornstarch with remaining water; add to pan and bring to boil. Remove from heat, add lemon juice and cool. Makes 2/3 cup.

PUMPKIN CARAMEL CUSTARD

2 tablespoons medium molasses	1 1/2 cups (or 1 13-ounce can,) evaporated milk
1 tablespoon honey	
5 large eggs	1/2 teaspoon salt
1 cup cooked canned pumpkin	1 teaspoon ground cinnamon
1/3 cup water	1/8 teaspoon ground cloves
1/4 cup honey	
1/4 cup medium molasses	1 1/2 teaspoons vanilla extract

Put 2 tablespoons molasses and 1 tablespoon honey in bottom of an 8-inch round cake pan. Put into a 400° F. oven and bake for 7 to 10 minutes. When ready, huge bubbles will be rising in the pan. Remove pan from oven and set aside for a few minutes for "caramel" to harden. Meanwhile break eggs into a bowl and whisk until foamy. Add remaining ingredients and whisk to mix well. Pour mixture (about 4 3/4 cups) into caramel-lined cake pan. Carefully set pan in another, slightly larger pan, such as a roasting pan. Fill larger pan with water to about 1/2-inch below top of pudding-filled pan. (This water-jacket will insulate pumpkin custard, prevent it from curdling while baking). Put into a 350° F. oven and bake 55 to 60 minutes until custard is firm in center. Remove cake pan from water-jacket; cool, then chill. Run a knife around edge of pumpkin custard; put a large serving plate upside down on top and turn them quickly over together. Custard will fall out and caramel run over it as a sauce. Cut like a cake to serve. Serves 8 or more.

NATURAL RICE PUDDING, ENGLISH STYLE

This is made without eggs. I may be prejudiced but I find this much more interesting than little bits of rice lost in a custard coating.

Rice pudding can be served alone or with kissel, fruit sauce or poached fruit such as plums, apples or rhubarb. If the pudding is flavored with cinnamon, ground cinnamon can be sprinkled on just before serving. Or, you can add 1/4 cup raisins or currants to the pudding with the honey.

1/2 **cup short grain**
brown rice
2 1/2 **cups milk**
2 **tablespoons honey**

For *flavoring: vanilla pod,*
orange rind or cinnamon
stick*

Put rice into a heavy 2- to 3-quart pan with milk and flavoring. Bring to a simmer, stir, then cover and cook over a very low heat for 1 hour. Stir in honey and cook, covered, 15 minutes longer. Rice will be slightly chewy. Add a little more milk if it seems dry. Serve warm or cold. Makes about 2 cups.

BARLEY PUDDING

Barley pudding can be flavored and served the same ways as rice pudding.

1/2 **cup hulled barley**
4 **cups milk**

2 **tablespoons honey**

Bring barley and milk to simmering point in a heavy 2- to 3-quart pan. Stir, then cover and simmer over low heat for 1 1/2 hours. Stir two or three times and add more milk if pudding seems too dry. Add honey to pudding and serve warm or cold. Makes 2 2/3 cups.

*For the flavoring use half a vanilla pod, or 2 2-inch strips of orange rind cut with a vegetable peeler, or a 3-inch cinnamon stick. Vanilla pod can be rinsed and dried after use and used again. The mass of tiny black seeds inside the pod provide the flavor; scrape about a quarter of a teaspoonful into the pudding.

BROWN BARLEY PUDDING

1 cup natural brown barley	*4 teaspoons honey*
3 cups cold water	*2 teaspoons rosewater (optional)*
Pinch salt	*1 to 2 tablespoons chopped*
1 1/2 cups evaporated milk	*pistachio nuts (optional)*

Bring barley and water to a simmer. Add salt. Cook, covered over medium heat until chewy tender, about 1 1/2 hours. Add more water if necessary. Add evaporated milk. Simmer, covered, 30 minutes longer. Stir in honey. Serve warm or cold, with rose water and pistachio nuts if you wish. Makes 2 cups. *Note:* the barley remains chewy, but good.

MONDAY RICE

Monday was washday during my childhood. The day started with a fire being lit under the built-in, round-bottomed, copper wash-boiler. After breakfast, a large rice pudding was put to bake untended in the kitchen range, while the piles of clothes were washed, scrubbed, boiled, starched, blued, and hung out to dry.

1/2 cup short grain brown rice	*2 1/4 cups milk*
1 tablespoon honey	*1 teaspoon butter*

Rinse rice in a strainer and put into a 1-quart casserole or baking dish. Drizzle honey over rice then pour in milk. Let butter float on top of milk. Bake pudding for 2 1/2 hours at 275° F. Rice will turn slightly brown and a delicious skin form on top. Add a little more milk if pudding seems too dry. Serve warm. Makes 2 cups. Serves 3 to 4.

‡ APPLE RICE (using leftover rice)

2 cups cooked brown
  rice*
4 tablespoons lemon
  juice
1/4 cup honey

1/4 cup heavy cream or
  evaporated milk
2 cups coarsely grated
  eating apples

Use rice that's been cooked only with water and salt. Mix first with lemon juice, then honey. Whip cream or evaporated milk (see directions on can). Stir a small spoonful into the rice then fold in the remainder. Grate apples, (no need to peel or core, just stop grating when you get to the core) and fold into rice. Serve at room temperature or chilled. Makes about 3 1/3 cups, serves 5 to 6.

ILLEGAL ICE CREAM

This dessert tastes more like ice milk than rich, creamy French vanilla ice cream but it's good. Why illegal? The U.S. government would never let you get away with selling this as ice cream which, by law must contain at least 10 percent butterfat. Make this dish only when you can be near the kitchen for about 3 hours.

1 cup water
1 tablespoon
  freeze-dried coffee†
1 cup instant nonfat
  dry milk

1 tablespoon oil,
  preferably soy bean
  oil
2 tablespoons honey
1 teaspoon vanilla
  extract

Whisk water with coffee in a deep metal, glass or plastic bowl. Add remaining ingredients and whisk again briefly. Put in freezer for 1 hour, or until ice crystals start to form around the edge. Whip mixture with a rotary beater, electric mixer or balloon whisk. Freeze 30 minutes longer. Whip again. Freeze 30 minutes

*Plain cooked barley or millet can be prepared the same way
†To make honey-vanilla ice cream, omit the coffee.

longer. Do this about 3 times more. When very thick and creamy, cover bowl and freeze until mixture is firm, at least 1 hour longer. Makes 2 cups. The air you whip in makes the ice cream smooth and increases the volume. The freezing and whipping can be done in an electric blender; after final whipping transfer mixture to a container to freeze firm.

YEASTED WHOLE-WHEAT APPLE CAKE

1/2 cup apple cider or apple juice	1/2 teaspoon salt
2 envelopes or 2 tablespoons dry yeast	1/4 pound (1 stick) sweet butter, at room temperature
3/4 cup honey	1 cup rolled oats
1 egg	1 cup raisins
1 1/4 cups whole-wheat flour	1/2 cup coarsely chopped walnuts, filberts or pecans
1 teaspoon cinnamon	1 cup finely chopped apple, peeled or
1/16 teaspoon ground cloves	unpeeled

Turn oven on at "warm" for 5 minutes, then turn off. Meanwhile, warm apple cider or juice in a 2 1/2- to 3-quart pan. When lukewarm, remove from heat and stir in yeast and honey with a wooden spoon. Let stand 2 to 3 minutes. Add egg, whole-wheat flour, cinnamon, cloves, salt and sweet butter; stir until smooth and well mixed. Stir in rolled oats, then beat the mixture for 2 minutes or about 100 strokes. Mix in raisins, nuts and apple. Pour into a buttered loaf pan, 9 x 5 x 3 inches, or 8 x 4 x 3 inches. Cover pan with plastic wrap or a cloth and set in warmed oven for 1 hour. Mixture will rise very slightly. Remove cover, turn oven on and set thermostat to 350° F. Bake for 1 hour and 10 minutes. When done, center will be springy to the touch and cake will start to shrink from sides of pan. Run a knife around edge to loosen cake. Set pan on a rack for 30 minutes before turning cake out onto rack. Serve warm or cold. Cake keeps well, wrapped and refrigerated. Makes about 18 slices.

YOGURT COTTAGE CHEESE CAKE

This is very moist and light, like a cheese cake without the crust.

1 cup plain yogurt	1/4 teaspoon salt
2 cups (1 pound) creamed cottage cheese, large or small curd	1/4 teaspoon grated lemon rind
1/2 cup honey	1 tablespoon lemon juice
1/4 cup cornstarch	4 eggs, separated
2 teaspoons vanilla extract	

Put yogurt, cottage cheese, honey, cornstarch, vanilla extract and salt into an electric blender. Grate lemon rind on the finest side of the grater and be careful to take the yellow part only, as the white pith is bitter. Add grated rind and lemon juice to blender. "Separate" the eggs: crack one open and hold half the shell in each hand. Let the white drop into a clean, dry 3-quart bowl (for later beating) and tip the yolk from half-shell to half-shell until all the white has fallen off. Add the yolk to the blender. Repeat with remaining 3 eggs. Now turn on the blender and whir until mixture is smooth, about 2 minutes. Stop machine and scrape mixture from sides. Whir again briefly. Next, with a rotary beater or electric mixer, whip the egg whites* until very white and stiff. When they are stiff enough they will look something like puffy white clouds in the sky. Pour mixture from blender into egg whites. Then with a rubber spatula or metal spoon fold egg whites into cottage cheese mixture. To do this, cut across the center of the mixture with the spoon and turn the mixture over; at same time turn bowl slightly with other hand. Continue cutting, folding, and turning until the egg whites and cheese mixture are amalgamated. Pour mixture into an 8-inch square baking dish. Bake for 40 minutes at 325° F. Let cool thoroughly before cutting and serving from the pan. Serves 10 or more.

---

*Egg whites don't hold up more than 5 minutes or so after being whipped. So whenever you make a dish calling for stiffly beaten egg whites don't wander away after whipping them.

AUSTRIAN CURD CAKE

A moist cake about 1-inch high, with a delicious flavor.

4 tablespoons soft butter	1/3 cup farina, or cream of rice, or granulated tapioca
1/3 cup honey	
2 large eggs, separated	3 tablespoons lemon juice
1 1/2 cups (3/4 pound) creamed large curd cottage cheese	1/2 cup raisins

With a small balloon whisk, whisk butter and honey in a bowl. Separate the eggs: to do this, crack one open and hold half the shell in each hand. Let white drop into a clean, dry bowl for later beating, tip yolk from half-shell to half-shell until all the white has fallen off. Drop yolk into honey-butter mixture. Repeat with remaining egg. Whisk yolks into butter and honey, then whisk in cottage cheese, one half cup at a time. (Cottage cheese will remain in fairly large curds.) Whisk in farina, then mix in lemon juice and raisins. With an egg beater, whip egg whites until very stiff and white. (Whites will not whip properly if bowl is wet or greasy, or if there is yolk present. Beater must be clean and dry.) Stir a large spoonful of beaten whites into cottage-cheese mixture, then use a rubber scraper to cut and fold in the remainder. Pour batter into a lightly oiled 8-inch square baking pan. Bake for 50 minutes at 350° F. Cake will rise hardly at all. When baked, set pan on rack to cool. Serve warm or cold, straight from pan. Serves 6 to 8.

CRANBERRY CINNAMON OAT STREUSEL

Make one to two days before serving.

1/2 pound (2 1/2 cups) fresh or frozen cranberries*
1/4 cup honey
1 tablespoon cornstarch
1 tablespoon cold water
1 cup rolled oats
1/2 cup whole-wheat pastry flour or

regular whole-wheat flour
1/2 teaspoon ground cinnamon
4 tablespoons (1/2 stick) butter or margarine
2 tablespoons medium molasses
2 tablespoons honey

Rinse cranberries in a strainer and put in a pan. Add honey (but no water) and stir over medium heat until berries change color, but remain mostly whole, about 5 minutes. Mix cornstarch with cold water in a small bowl; stir into cranberries. Simmer 1 minute, remove from heat. Let cool while you prepare the streusel: mix rolled oats, whole-wheat pastry flour and cinnamon in a bowl. Add butter, cut into small pieces. Rub butter into flour and oats by scooping up mixture in each hand and rubbing it between thumb and fingers. Work quickly. When butter is worked in, drizzle honey and molasses over mixture. Mix all together with a fork; mixture will be sticky. Press half (1/2 cup) into bottom of an 8 x 4 x 2-inch loaf pan, preferably not metal. Spoon cranberry mixture over, then scatter remaining flour mixture over top in as small pieces as possible. Bake at 325° F. for 40 minutes, until top is browned. This dessert is best served cold, a day after it is made. Cut in slices and lift onto a plate, or serve straight from pan. Keeps a week in the refrigerator.

---

*This recipe also can be made with sour cherries, rhubarb, raspberries or soaked dried apricots.

CORN CRISP

Chewy, and keeps well. For a slightly "shorter" texture use 3/4 cup each corn meal and flour. Whole-wheat flour can be used instead of the unbleached white flour.

1/2 cup oil or soft
    butter, or a
    combination
1/3 cup medium
    molasses (blackstrap
    is too strong)
1 cup stone-ground
    coarse yellow corn
    meal

1/2 cup unbleached
    white flour
1 tablespoon soy
    granules, if
    available
2 tablespoons honey

Measure all ingredients into a bowl—or even directly into a nine-inch ungreased pie pan. Mash together thoroughly with the back of a wooden spoon then press flat in pie pan with spoon or fingers. Bake 20 minutes at 375° F. Set pan on rack for 10 minutes to cool. Cut into 12 wedges, then leave at least 20 minutes longer before removing from pan to rack to finish cooling. Makes 12 pieces.

WHEAT GERM, OATMEAL AND RAISIN COOKIES

2 eggs
1/2 cup nonfat dry milk
1 cup honey
2 tablespoons molasses
1/2 cup oil
2 teaspoons vanilla
    extract
1 teaspoon salt

1/2 cup raisins
1/2 cup walnuts
2 cups rolled oats, or
    wheat flakes or
    barley flakes
3/4 cup soy flour
1 1/2 cups wheat germ

Break eggs into a mixing bowl and whisk. Whisk in nonfat dry milk. Add honey, molasses, oil, vanilla extract and salt to bowl, then whisk them in, too. Dump raisins, walnuts, rolled oats, soy flour and wheat germ into bowl. Stir them in with a wooden spoon. Drop mixture in heaping teaspoonfuls on to a well-oiled cookie sheet. The cookies do not spread during baking so you can put them fairly close together. Bake for 10 to 15 minutes at 350° F. Remove from cookie sheet to a rack to cool. Cookies keep well in an airtight container. Makes about 56.

WHOLE-WHEAT PEANUT SQUARES

Soft and cakelike, with a very peanutty flavor.

1/4 cup (1/2 stick) butter at room temperature
1/4 cup peanut butter (4 tablespoons)
1/2 cup honey
1/4 cup medium molasses (blackstrap is too strong)
1 egg
1/4 cup milk
1/2 cup whole wheat pastry flour
1/2 cup toasted wheat germ

In a mixing bowl with a wooden spoon, beat butter with peanut butter for a few seconds. When smooth, add remaining ingredients and beat again. Spread mixture evenly in a well-greased 8-inch square baking pan. Bake for 35 minutes at 350° F., until top springs back when pressed lightly. Mixture will rise scarcely at all. When done, set pan on rack to cool. Cut into 16 squares or 24 rectangular "fingers." These keep well, stored in airtight container or frozen.

Variation: Add 1/4 cup chopped peanuts to the batter with the wheat germ.

‡ CHINESE SWEET BEAN PASTE

This delicious candy looks a little scary and because it's black people expect the taste of licorice. Decorate the paste if you wish with a pignolia or pistachio nut on each wedge.

> 1 cup black beans
> 3 cups water
> 1/2 cup honey

> 1/4 cup oil, preferably peanut oil

Soak beans in cold water for from 8 to 24 hours in refrigerator. Bring to boil in same water in a heavy 2- to 3-quart pot. Cook covered until tender, about 1 hour. Drain. Put honey and oil in electric blender. Add beans and whir until you have a smooth paste—stopping the machine and pushing mixture down once or twice. Put mixture back into pot beans were cooked in. Stir over medium high heat for about 10 minutes until very stiff and coming away from sides of pan. Heat needs to be high enough so mixture bubbles, but not so high that it scorches. When done, turn paste onto a board. When cool enough to handle, shape into two cakes, each about 1/2 inch thick. Cut into wedges. Serve as dessert or candy. Makes 1 1/2 cups paste. Keeps well in the refrigerator.

Red Bean Paste: Bring 1 cup aduki beans to boil in a heavy 2- to 3-quart pot. Simmer covered for 1 hour. Then follow recipe for black bean paste. (Aduki beans are small, red, and sweet tasting; they do not require preliminary soaking.)

DATE AND WALNUT CANDY

> 1/2 cup rolled oats
> 1/2 pound (about 20) dates, pitted

> 1 cup (4 ounces) shelled walnuts

Put oats through a meat grinder about 1 tablespoon at a time. (If you pour them all in at once, grinder handle simply will not turn.) When done, grind dates and walnuts. Work oats, dates and nuts together with your hands until well mixed. Mixture will be quite stiff. Form into small balls, each about a heaping teaspoon-ful. Makes about 1 1/2 cups mixture, 35 to 40 balls. Covered and refrigerated, the candy keeps well.

‡ CARROT HALVA

In India, halvas (meaning "sweet mixtures") are offered with tea to guests. Indians cook this halva until it's dry and crumbly. When, as here, honey is used instead of sugar, the mixture is sticky, but the flavor is equally good.

> 3 **cups coarsely grated carrots**
> 1 **can (about 13 fluid ounces) evaporated milk**
> 1/4 **cup honey**
> 2 **tablespoons medium**

> **molasses (blackstrap is too strong)**
> 1 **tablespoon butter**
> **Seeds from 2 cardamom pods, or, 1/4 teaspoon ground cardamom**

Put carrots, evaporated milk, honey and molasses in a heavy 2- to 3-quart pot. Bring just to simmering point then simmer, uncovered, over low heat for 1 hour. Add butter and turn up heat so mixture boils. Stir constantly; you will be chained to the stove for about 30 minutes. Mixture will gradually thicken and darken as the liquid evaporates. Watch carefully, so mixture does not scorch; lower heat if necessary. When mixture is very, very stiff, quite dark in color, and comes away from sides of pan, remove from heat.* Grind cardamom seeds in a small mortar, (or between paper with a rolling pin). Stir ground cardamom into halva. Cool before serving. Serve in a bowl. Pick up with fingers to eat. Makes between 1 1/4 and 1 1/3 cups. Keeps at least one week in the refrigerator.

*If you are uncertain as to when mixture is ready, measure it. If you have between 1 1/4 and 1 1/3 cups, you're there.

8

---⌣---

Make Your Own...

Bread

Good bread, made with first-class ingredients, makes a real contribution to family pleasure and nutrition. The flavor, texture and nutritional value of homemade bread is vastly superior to most commercial kinds. To make nutritious breads you need nutritious flours—preferably whole grain—that have been ground as recently as possible and stored in a cool place. Whole-grain flours have better quality protein and more of it than refined flour; they also have a plentiful supply of many more vitamins and minerals. When white flour is used, a little added wheat germ gives some whole grain value. Soy flour and nonfat dry milk are included in most of the yeast bread recipes in this book to upgrade the quality and quantity of the protein in the finished loaf.

If you've never made bread before, please read all the introductory material first, because an informed breadmaker is usually a happy breadmaker. Almost all the yeast bread recipes in this book are made by exactly the same method, a speedy, effecient method that uses as little equipment as possible. Once you've got the hang of it, you won't have to pore over different instructions each time you try a new bread.

The first time or two that you bake bread, go slowly and allow yourself plenty of time. Many people think of breadmaking as a mysterious process. In fact, bread dough is very amenable. It doesn't need exact, to-the-minute care and attention—as long as you respect certain limits.

Once you feel confident, adapt breadmaking to your way of life. Say you're planning to go marketing for 2 hours. Make up the dough, using lukewarm water, and leave it in a cool place, instead of a warm one, to rise—even in the refrigerator will work. You may also cut the yeast by half, as this, too, will slow down the rising.

If you're in a hurry and want to speed up the rising, turn the oven on "warm" while you make up and knead the dough. Then, turn off the oven and put in the covered bowl of dough; in 20 to 30 minutes it will have risen enough. You can also double the quantity of yeast called for, although the bread will taste yeastier.

If you let dough rise too long at too high a temperature, it will develop a sour, fermented flavor. So, if the dough is well-risen but you are not yet ready to shape and bake it, punch the dough down in the bowl with your fist. Cover as before and leave it alone; the dough will slowly rise again. You can repeat this rising-and-punching-down two or three times; in fact many bakers feel that bread dough should always rise at least twice.

If you are out of the house all day, then try this method developed by the best-known yeast company: make up dough and knead. Leave it on the board, cover with plastic wrap, and turn the bowl in which you made the dough upside down on top of it. Let stand for 20 minutes. Knead again briefly, shape, and put into greased loaf pans or onto metal baking (cookie) sheets. Cover loosely with plastic wrap. Refrigerate for 2 to 24 hours. When ready to bake, remove bread from refrigerator. Uncover dough carefully. Let stand uncovered for 10 minutes at room temperature while oven heats. Puncture any bubbles on the dough's surface with a toothpick or skewer. Bake at 400° F. for 30 to 40 minutes. Cool on rack.

I tried several of the bread recipes in this book with this method. I found it works fine, though the finished loaves are slightly smaller and the bread denser than when made by the regular methods.

BREADMAKING TECHNIQUE (the reason behind the actions specified in each recipe)

1. "In a large bowl, mix the water, yeast and honey." I almost always make up the dough in my large 6-quart enameled iron pot. It's thick and heavy and keeps the dough snug while rising. Besides, instead of covering the rising dough with a towel or plastic you can simply put the lid on the pot. If you use a bowl, any kind —plastic, metal or crockery—will do.

Yeast, compressed or dried, is in a dormant state when you buy it. Given water, food (honey and flour) and warmth it springs into action and starts to multiply. Bubbles of carbon dioxide are a by-product of the reproduction process and it's these gas bubbles which cause the dough to expand. To get the yeast started, and warm up the whole dough, the water called for in the recipes should be very warm, 105 to 115° F. That is higher than your blood temperature (98.4° F) but much lower than boiling point (212° F). If you don't have a thermometer, use your hand; the water should feel comfortably hot.

After you have mixed the honey, yeast and water, and before you start measuring in the flours, TAKE A GOOD LOOK AT THE YEAST MIXTURE TO MAKE SURE THE YEAST IS ALIVE AND WORKING. The granules of dried yeast should be swelling slightly, losing their granular look and becoming creamy. The mixture should also smell yeasty. (When using compressed yeast, first mix it with the honey in the bowl and then add the water. As you mix it with the honey the yeast will be runny and creamy.) You should be able to tell within a minute whether the yeast is okay. If it isn't, if nothing happens, you need to begin again with fresh yeast.

The total 5-minute wait suggested in each recipe before you stir in the flours can be cut short if you're really rushed, but it is better to give the yeast a headstart on honey before you burden it with a mass of flour.

2. "Add remaining ingredients to bowl in order given." When included in a bread recipe in this book, nonfat dry milk powder is added first, so it can dissolve properly in the water. If mixed dry with the flour, the milk may remain undissolved all the way.

Many bread recipes call for two bowls—one in which the yeast is dissolved and another for the flour. But it's perfectly all right to measure the other ingredients right into the yeast and honey while it is "brewing." Just don't mix them in until the time is up, and the process will go on without the use of extra bowls.

Once the milk is in, the flours come next. They should be at room temperature. All the recipes in this book have been made with flour measured either by scooping it out of a huge bagful with the measuring cup, or pouring it from the sack straight into the measuring cup. Don't pack the flour down in the cup and always level off the top with a spatula or finger.

There is no need to sift grain flour when making bread; sift soy flour or *non*-instant dry milk powder only if they are lumpy. Use a large strainer; one 6 to 8 inches in diameter is useful for many kitchen tasks. A flour sifter is a completely unnecessary gadget.

3. "Stir in with spoon, then switch to using one hand instead." No special reason for this—I like to do it this way and it just seems the simplest way.

4. "Add more flour if the mixture is very sticky." Because flours vary in their ability to absorb liquid according to their genetic traits, age and the humidity of storage places, it is not possible to accurately specify how much flour is needed. In almost every recipe you will probably need to use at least half a cup more flour. One day a particular recipe will require 6 cups of flour and the next time it will absorb 7 cups. "Enough" is when the dough is no longer wet-sticky on the outside. The amount can be adjusted further while you are kneading the dough. Don't worry about the exact degree of dryness; it isn't crucial to the finished loaf.

5. "Turn the dough onto a floured board." At this stage the dough will be quite raggy looking and need not even be thoroughly mixed. If sticky, add more flour during kneading until the dough sticks neither to your hands nor to a lightly floured board. The "board" can just as easily be a plastic surface. It should not, however, be a chilling surface such as stainless steel or marble.

6. "Knead until smooth and silky." Next to taking your own bread from the oven and eating it, kneading is the most satisfying part of breadmaking. As you read these instructions, if you've never made bread before, practice by using a small towel or a piece of cloth on a slippery surface.

To knead: Work with both hands. With fingertips, lift up the edge of the dough farthest away from you and bend it toward the center of the dough. Just as you are about to press the edge down into the center of the dough catch the edge with the *palms* of your hands and press hard down and away from you. As you press the dough down and away from you, turn it very slightly clockwise.

Then lift up the edge of the dough farthest away from you again and repeat the process. Keep going—developing a speedy, steady rhythm: pick up, bend forward, press down-and-away, turn slightly, pick up, bend forward, etc. When you do the press-down-and-away bit, put the weight of your whole body behind that press. Kneading is not a light delicate fingering.

As you knead (and this is why you knead) you exercise the gluten in the flour. When the dough has become stretchy, elastic and silky in feeling, keep kneading a minute or two longer to fully develop the gluten. Kneading gives bread the desirable texture, making it "pully" with "a good tooth," not cakelike.

If you have an electric mixer, of course, you can use the dough hook attachment to knead the dough. It saves a lot of good-feeling exertion! And you miss out on the pleasure of feeling a raggy heap of dough change into something soft, silky and elastic in your own hands.

7. "Put back in bowl, smooth side up." There is no need to wash out the bowl. However if the room is cool or you want the dough to rise quickly, fill the bowl with very hot water, let it stand while you are kneading the dough, then quickly wash, rinse, and dry it before putting the dough back in.

"Smooth side up" simply means that the seam where you have been pressing down each time goes on the bottom of the bowl as it will later go on the baking sheet or in a loaf pan.

8. "Cover with a damp cloth, or with plastic." Dough rises best in a warm, humid atmosphere. The best and easiest way to arrange this is to put the whole bowl in a large plastic bag, creating a miniature greenhouse. Use the same bag over and over again. A damp towel works well, but can be frustrating to organize, and leaves you with a soggy towel.

9. "Let rise." Put the bowl containing the dough in a warm room or any warm place around 75 to 80° F. High up in the kitchen (such as on top of the refrigerator) can be good, or a warm damp bathroom. Or set the bowl in a large container of hot

water. One of the best and simplest ways to arrange a warm atmosphere is to turn the oven on at "warm" for 5 minutes before you start making the dough, and then turn it off; when the dough is kneaded, put the bowl in the warm oven.

10. "Until double in bulk." There is a very simple test for this. Press two fingers about 1/2 inch into the dough. If the indentations remain, your dough is ready.

11. "Turn dough back onto board and knead again." Do this to press out most of the air bubbles that have formed and to further exercise the gluten. This second kneading can be brief. If the dough has risen but for some reason you are not ready to shape and bake it, simply punch the dough down hard in the bowl with your fist and let it rise again.

12. "Knead each piece briefly and shape into a round loaf." I personally don't bother with bread pans. Shaping the dough into a round loaf is quick, simple, and results in a larger proportion of delicious crust, although there is some extra loss of thiamin, a B vitamin. But if you are making 6 or more loaves at a time, as many people do, then pans are your best choice because you can get 6 or 8 in the oven at once, which you cannot do with space-consuming round loaves. You can use bread pans in any of the recipes here (all have been tried with pans) using either the 9 x 5 x 3 inch size or the 8 x 4 x 2 inch. Different recipes will produce different-sized loaves.

It doesn't really matter how you shape the loaf—oval, round, or braided, it's up to you.

13. "Set on baking sheet sprinkled with corn meal." Corn meal prevents sticking. You can use cheap, degerminated corn meal (it's a waste to use good stone ground), or alternatively, you can spread a thin film of oil or butter over the baking sheet with a piece of rag or paper towel. Many cooks feel that bread sticks to oil, but I have never found this a problem.

14. "Cover as before and let rise again until double." Use same plastic covering you used before, and make the same two-finger test for "double." The second rising usually takes about 30 minutes.

15. "Bake." The oven is always preheated—allow about 10 minutes to reach desired temperature. Ovens vary, some thermostats are as much as 20 to 25 degrees off in either direction; a

service man can correct this condition. It's best to have an oven thermometer and use it to check the oven occasionally. Adjust the temperature if necessary to allow for any differences.

Most of the following bread recipes call for baking time of 10 to 15 minutes at 400° F. followed by about 20 minutes at 350° F. If you don't plan to be near the kitchen while the loaves are baking you may like to try baking them for 40 to 45 minutes at 375° F. Or, just before the second rising is finished, in your estimation, put the dough in an *unheated* oven. Turn on the oven and set to 350° F. Baking time then will be almost 1 hour.

No matter how you bake it, bread is a good rich color when it is done. To check for doneness, pick up a loaf with a cloth, turn it upside down, and tap the bottom. If the sound is "hollow," the bread is baked.

Put the loaves, whether baked in a pan or on cookie sheets, on a rack to cool. Cool bread cuts better and usually tastes better, though sometimes you just can't wait that long to sample it.

16. To store, keep bread in a cool, but not airtight place. If keeping for more than a day or two, put loaf in a plastic bag in the refrigerator (use same bag over and over). Don't put it in plastic before it has cooled, or it will lose its crustiness. All breads, well-wrapped, freeze beautifully. They should be quite, quite cold before being frozen. If you have the freezer space, once you've got the hang of breadmaking, you can double or triple the recipes.

The Ingredients

YEAST

Yeast is available in dry form, or compressed with starch into a moist cake. The dry kind comes in individual, moisture-proof envelopes, or in a vacuum-packed jar, or in bulk in plastic bags. Dry yeast keeps well on a cool, dry pantry shelf or in an airtight, moisture-proof container in the refrigerator.

Each kind of yeast can be used interchangeably: Use one envelope (1/4 ounce) dry yeast, or one scant tablespoon from jar or plastic bag, or about 3/5 ounce compressed yeast.

Chilling or freezing yeast or yeast dough retards its growth but does not kill it. Too high a temperature does kill the yeast, which is what happens when you bake the bread dough.

FLOUR

Because it contains more gluten than most other flours, wheat flour is basic to breadmaking. When the flour is mixed with water, stirred and kneaded, the gluten becomes stretchy and forms an elastic framework to enclose bubbles of gas produced by the yeast. High temperatures used in baking kill the yeast, and "set" the gluten.

Whole-wheat flour is more nutritious than white and comes in several different grinds which can be used interchangeably. Check the package to make sure the flour has not been bromated. Some stores sell flour especially for bread, ground from "hard" wheats which have more gluten than "soft" wheats used for cake flour. Whole-wheat flour does not have as a high a proportion of gluten as white, therefore the resulting bread has a crumblier texture. Knead whole-wheat dough thoroughly to develop the gluten as much as possible.

Barley, millet, rye and oat flours are low in gluten, therefore most recipes using them call for a proportion of unbleached white or whole-wheat flour. Bread made entirely of barley flour, for instance, comes out doughy and dense. When you use white flour, make sure it's unbleached.

The fresher the flour, the more nutritious the bread. Buy from a store that grinds it own, or has a fast turnover. Ideally, flour should be kept cool to slow down nutrient loss. Warm it to room temperature before mixing with yeast and water.

MILK

For ease and economy, use nonfat dry milk powder. In these bread recipes use either instant or non-instant dry milk interchangeably. Sift non-instant if it is lumpy, but storing it in an airtight container should avoid the necessity.

If you like, use fresh milk instead of the water in these recipes. Pasteurized milk needs only to be warmed. If you are using raw milk in these recipes, bring just to boiling point, then let cool.

When the yeast is added, the temperature of the milk or water should be 105 to 115° F.

SOY FLOUR

Soy flour, (as well as dry milk) increases the quantity and quality of protein in the bread. But too much soy makes a sticky bread and adversely affects the flavor. Usually, not more than 20 percent of the flour in a recipe can be soy. Use full fat or low fat soy flour. If you don't have soy flour, you can substitute an equal amount of wheat flour in these recipes.

OIL

Use corn, soy, safflower or any ordinary oil. Sesame oil, tahini, olive, or peanut oil can be used, but, generally speaking, bread is not good with flavored oils such as these.

WHEAT GERM, RICE BRAN, RICE POLISH, WHEAT BRAN, WHEAT GERM-AND-MIDDLINGS

These all contain valuable whole-grain nutrients. In a recipe calling for 6 to 7 cups of flour (especially white flour, from which many nutrients have been removed) you can replace 1 cup of the flour with 1 cup of any of the above. When you buy them, be sure that these ingredients are not rancid; store them in a cool place or in the refrigerator to avoid nutrient loss.

SWEETENERS

When using honey, a simple inexpensive blend is fine, though you can experiment with the more exotic honeys if you like. Molasses is good in dark breads (rye, whole-wheat, and even oatmeal), but in light breads the flavor is too strong and gets tiresome after a few slices. Malt syrup isn't exactly a sweetener, and when hop-flavored, it is almost bitter. But I like to use it in dark breads such as rye or pumpernickel and in whole-wheat and sprouted wheat bread. Use twice as much malt syrup as the honey called for.

VARIATIONS

Sesame, poppy, celery or caraway seeds, add interest, decoration and flavor to breads. Just before putting the bread in the oven, brush the top lightly with beaten egg, or egg white, and sprinkle with one kind of seed.

To any basic bread dough, you can add nuts, raisins, or dates and make delicious sweet breads. A mixture of almonds and cut-up apricots is good too.

Many people like to add ground seeds to bread. In a recipe that calls for 6 cups of flour, substitute 1 to 2 cups ground sesame or pumpkin seeds for 1 to 2 cups flour. Some health food stores sell sesame meal or pumpkin-seed meal. However, it's best to make your own, fresh, by whirring hulled seeds in an electric blender just before adding to the dough.

Menu-Makers Guide

Very Basic Breads for Daily Use:

  ‡ Cornell Whole-Wheat Bread
    Cornell Bread

Still Pretty Basic:

  ‡ Sprouted Wheat Bread
  ‡ Aztec Corn Bread
  ‡ Raisin Rye
    Walnut-Date Barley Bread
    Millet (or Cracked Wheat) Bread
    Oatmeal Bread
    Unyeasted Whole-Wheat Bread

Special, and very good:

  ‡ Cottage Cheese Dill Bread
  ‡ Chestnut Filbert Apple Bread
    Raisin Oatmeal Sticky Bread

Flatbreads, unleavened:

  ‡ Oatcakes
    Armenian Sesame Crisp Bread
  ‡ Corn Pone

‡ CORNELL WHOLE-WHEAT BREAD

3 cups very warm
  water
1 envelope or 1
  tablespoon dry yeast
2 tablespoons honey
3/4 cup nonfat dry milk
  powder
1 cup soy flour, sifted
  if lumpy

3 teaspoons (1
  tablespoon) salt
About 6 cups
  whole-wheat flour
2 tablespoons oil or
  soft butter

In a large bowl, mix water, yeast and honey with a wooden spoon. Let stand 5 minutes. Meanwhile add remaining ingredients to bowl in order given, but don't stir until the 5 minutes are up. Now stir the mixture with the wooden spoon. As soon as it is too stiff to stir, switch to using one hand instead. Add more whole-wheat flour if necessary to make a stiff dough that comes away from the side of the bowl. Turn the dough out onto a well-floured board and knead until smooth and silky, 3 to 5 minutes. As you knead, work in more flour if dough is still very sticky. Put dough, smooth side up, back in the bowl. Cover with a damp cloth or with plastic. Let rise until double in bulk, about 1 hour. Turn dough back onto floured board and knead it again briefly. Cut in half. Knead each piece briefly and shape into a round loaf; set on a baking sheet which has been sprinkled with cornmeal or lightly greased. Cover as before and let rise again until doubled. Bake for 15 minutes at 400° F., turn heat down to 350° F. and bake for 30 minutes longer. Slide loaves onto a rack to cool. Makes 2 loaves, about 1 1/2 pounds each.

CORNELL BREAD

This is "white" bread, with some whole-grain value from the wheat germ. The bread is not pure white in color, but rather has a golden crumb.

Until you can locate a source for soy flour you can omit it and replace with the same amount of unbleached white flour. The soy flour and the

nonfat dry milk improve the protein value of this basic everyday loaf, so soy
flour is worth hunting for.

3 cups very warm water	1 cup wheat germ
1 envelope or 1 tablespoon dry yeast	3 teaspoons (1 tablespoon) salt
2 tablespoons honey	About 4 1/2 cups unbleached white flour
1 cup nonfat dry milk powder	2 tablespoons oil or soft butter
1 cup soy flour, sifted if lumpy	

In a large bowl, mix water, yeast and honey with a wooden
spoon. Let stand 5 minutes. Meanwhile add remaining ingredients to bowl in order given, but don't stir in until the 5 minutes
are up. Now, stir the mixture with the wooden spoon. As soon as
it is too stiff to stir, switch to using one hand instead. Add more
white flour if necessary to make a stiff dough that comes away
from the side of the bowl. Turn the dough onto a well-floured
board and knead until smooth and silky, 3 to 5 minutes. As you
knead, work in more unbleached white flour if dough is still very
sticky. Put dough, smooth side up, back in the bowl. Cover with
a damp cloth or with plastic. Let rise until double in bulk, about
1 hour. Turn dough back onto floured board and knead it again
briefly. Cut in half. Knead each piece briefly and shape into a
round loaf; set on a baking sheet which has been sprinkled with
corn meal or lightly greased. Cover as before and let rise again
until doubled. Bake for 15 minutes at 400° F.; turn heat down to
350° F. and bake for 30 minutes longer. Slide loaves onto a rack
to cool. Makes 2 loaves about 1 1/2 pounds each.

‡ SPROUTED WHEAT BREAD

*Our favorite bread. Sprouted wheat grains are ground up and mixed with
the dough. Set the grain to sprout (see page 174) about 3 days before
making the bread.*

3 cups sprouted wheat
  (page 174), 1 cup
  kernels before
  sprouting
3 cups very warm
  water
1 envelope or 1
  tablespoon dry yeast
2 tablespoons honey

3/4 cup nonfat dry milk
  powder
3/4 cup soy flour, sifted
  if lumpy
1 teaspoon salt
About 6 cups unbleached
  white flour
1 tablespoon oil or
  soft butter.

Whir wheat sprouts in an electric blender with 1 cup of water.*
Put into a pan, stir over heat until boiling; set aside. In a large
bowl, mix remaining 2 cups water, the yeast and honey with a
wooden spoon. Let stand 5 minutes. Meanwhile add remaining
ingredients to bowl in order given, but don't stir in until the 5
minutes are up. Now add the wheat sprouts and stir the mixture
with the wooden spoon. As soon as the mixture is too stiff to stir,
switch to using one hand instead. Add more unbleached white
flour if necessary to make a stiff dough that comes away from the
side of the bowl. Turn dough out onto a well-floured board and
knead until smooth and silky, 3 to 5 minutes. As you knead, work
in more flour if dough is still very sticky. Put dough, smooth side
up, back in the bowl. Cover with a damp cloth or with plastic. Let
rise until double in bulk, about 1 hour. Turn dough back onto
floured board and knead it again briefly. Cut in half. Knead each
piece briefly and shape into a round loaf; set on a baking sheet
which has been lightly sprinkled with corn meal or lightly
greased. Cover as before and let rise again until doubled. Bake
for 40 minutes at 350° F. Slide loaves onto a rack to cool. Makes
2 loaves, about 1 pound 6 ounces each.

Or put sprouts through a meat grinder, then heat with 1 cup of the water.

‡ AZTEC CORN BREAD

2 1/2 *cups stone ground*
     whole yellow corn
     meal, undegermed
   3 *cups very hot water*
   1 *envelope or 1*
     tablespoon dry yeast
1/3 *cup nonfat dry milk*
     powder

1/2 *cup soy flour, sifted*
     if lumpy
   2 *teaspoons salt*
About 4 1/2 *cups*
     whole-wheat flour

In a large bowl, mix corn meal and water with a wooden spoon. Corn meal will cool water. When mixture is just very warm, stir in yeast. Let stand 5 minutes. Meanwhile add remaining ingredients to bowl in order given, but don't stir in until the 5 minutes are up. Now stir the mixture with the wooden spoon. As soon as it is too stiff to stir, switch to using one hand instead. Add more whole-wheat flour if necessary to make a stiff dough that comes away from the side of the bowl. Turn the dough out onto a well-floured board and knead until smooth and silky, 3 to 5 minutes. As you knead, work in more flour if dough is still very sticky. Put dough, smooth side up, back in the bowl. Cover with a damp cloth or with plastic. Let rise until double in bulk, about 1 hour. Turn dough onto floured board and knead it again briefly. Cut in half, knead each piece briefly and shape into a round loaf; set on a baking sheet which has been lightly sprinkled with corn meal. Cover as before and let rise again until doubled. Bake for 10 minutes at 400° F., turn heat down to 350° F. and bake for 30 minutes longer. Slide loaves onto a rack to cool. Makes 2 loaves, about 1 pound 10 ounces each.

‡ RAISIN RYE BREAD

3 cups very warm
water
2 envelopes or 2
tablespoons dried
yeast
1/4 cup molasses or malt
syrup
1/4 cup honey
1/2 cup nonfat dry milk
powder

1/2 cup soy flour, sifted
if lumpy
2 1/2 teaspoons salt
2 tablespoons oil or
soft butter
About 3 cups rye flour
About 3 cups whole-wheat
flour
6 cups (1 1/2 pounds)
raisins

In a large bowl, mix the water, yeast, molasses and honey with a wooden spoon. Let stand 5 minutes. Meanwhile add remaining ingredients, except raisins, to bowl in order given, but don't stir in until the 5 minutes are up. Now stir the mixture with the wooden spoon. As soon as it is too stiff to stir, switch to using one hand instead. Add more whole wheat and rye flour if necessary to make a stiff dough that comes away from the side of the bowl. Turn dough out onto a well-floured board. Knead until smooth and silky, 3 to 5 minutes. As you knead, work in more flour if dough is still very sticky. Put dough, smooth side up, back in the bowl. Cover with a damp cloth or with plastic. Let rise until double in bulk, about 1 hour. Turn dough back onto floured board and knead it again briefly while working in raisins. Cut in half, knead each piece briefly and shape into a cylindrical loaf, about 10-inches long; set on a baking sheet which has been lightly sprinkled with corn meal or lightly greased. Cover as before and let rise again until doubled. Bake for 15 minutes at 400° F., then turn heat down to 350° F. and bake 35 minutes longer. Put loaves on rack to cool. Makes 2 loaves, each about 1 3/4 pounds.

WALNUT DATE BARLEY BREAD

3 cups very warm water	2 teaspoons salt
1 tablespoon honey	About 2 cups (7 ounces) barley flour
1 envelope or 1 tablespoon dry yeast	About 3 1/2 cups unbleached white flour
1/2 cup nonfat dry milk powder	1 1/2 cups cut-up pitted dates
1/2 cup soy flour, sifted if lumpy	1 1/2 cups broken-up walnut meats
1/2 cup wheat germ	

In a large bowl, mix water, honey, and yeast with a wooden spoon. Let stand 5 minutes. Meanwhile add remaining ingredients, except for dates and walnuts, to bowl in the order given, but don't stir until the 5 minutes are up. Now stir the mixture with the wooden spoon. As soon as it is too stiff to stir, switch to using one hand instead. Add more barley and white flour if necessary, to make a stiff dough that comes away from the side of the bowl. Turn dough onto a well-floured board. Knead until smooth and silky, 3 to 5 minutes. As you knead, work in more flour if dough is still very sticky. Put dough, smooth side up, back in the bowl. Cover with a damp cloth or with plastic. Let rise until double in bulk, about 1 hour. Turn dough back onto floured board and knead it again briefly. Work in the walnuts and dates. Cut dough in half. Knead each piece briefly and shape into a round loaf; set on a baking sheet which has been lightly sprinkled with corn meal or lightly greased. Cover as before and let rise again until doubled. Bake for 10 minutes at 400° F., then turn heat down to 325° F. and bake 25 minutes longer. Slide loaves onto a rack to cool. Makes 2 loaves, about 1 1/2 pounds each.

MILLET BREAD

The millet flavor is very faint, particularly if it is combined with whole-wheat flour. But bread is a pleasant way to include millet in family menus.

1/2 cup (4 ounces)   1 tablespoon honey
    hulled millet*   1/2 cup nonfat dry milk
1 1/2 cups boiling water   powder
About 3 cups unbleached   1/2 cup soy flour, sifted
    white or   if lumpy
    whole-wheat flour   1 1/2 teaspoons salt
    1 envelope or 1   1 tablespoon oil or
    tablespoon dry yeast   soft butter

Whir millet in electric blender until fine; it will remain slightly gritty. Put in large bowl and pour the boiling water over it. Let stand 5 minutes. Stir in 1 cup of the whole-wheat or white flour with a wooden spoon; mixture should now be just very warm. Stir in yeast and honey. Let stand 5 minutes. Meanwhile add remaining ingredients to bowl in order given, but don't stir them in until the 5 minutes are up. Now stir the mixture with the wooden spoon. As soon as it is too stiff to stir, switch to using one hand instead. Add more whole-wheat or white flour if necessary to make a stiff dough that comes away from the side of the bowl. Turn the dough out onto a well-floured board. Knead until smooth and silky, 3 to 5 minutes. As you knead, work in more flour if dough is still very sticky. Put dough, smooth side up, back in the bowl. Cover with a damp cloth or with plastic. Let rise again until double in bulk, about 1 hour. Turn dough back onto floured board and knead it again, briefly. Shape into a round loaf; set on a baking sheet which has been lightly sprinkled with corn meal or lightly greased. Cover as before and let rise again until doubled. Bake for 15 minutes at 400° F., turn heat down to 350° F. and bake for 30 minutes longer. Slide loaf onto a rack to cool. Makes 1 loaf, about 1 3/4 pounds.

Cracked Wheat Bread: Make as for millet bread using 1/2 cup coarse or medium bulgur instead of the millet. *Do not grind up the bulgur.* Pour the hot water over it and let stand 5 minutes. Instead of 3 cups whole-wheat flour, use 2 cups whole-wheat and 1 cup unbleached white. Makes 1 loaf about 1 3/4 pounds.

If you can obtain millet flour, use 1 cup plus 2 tablespoons instead of the hulled millet. Mix the yeast and honey with 1 1/2 cups very warm water and let stand 5 minutes. Add the millet flour with the wheat flour.

OATMEAL BREAD

1 cup rolled oats
2 cups hot water
1 envelope or 1
tablespoon dry yeast
1/2 cup honey or
molasses, or 1/4
cup each
3/4 cup nonfat dry milk
powder

1 cup soy flour, sifted
if lumpy
2 teaspoons salt
About 4 cups whole-wheat
or unbleached white
flour

In a large bowl, mix oats and hot water with a wooden spoon. Let stand 5 minutes. Mix in yeast, and molasses or honey. Let stand 3 minutes longer. Meanwhile add remaining ingredients to bowl in order given, but don't stir them until the 3 minutes are up. Now stir the mixture with the wooden spoon. As soon as it is too stiff to stir, switch to using one hand instead. Add more white or whole-wheat flour if necessary, to make a stiff dough that comes away from the side of the bowl. Turn the dough out onto a well-floured board. Knead until smooth and silky, 3 to 5 minutes. As you knead, work in more flour if dough is still very sticky. Put dough, smooth side up, back in the bowl. Cover with damp cloth or with plastic. Let rise until double in bulk, about 1 hour. Turn dough back onto floured board and knead again briefly. Cut in half. Knead each piece briefly and shape into a round loaf; set on a baking sheet which has been lightly sprinkled with corn meal or lightly greased. Cover as before and let rise again until doubled. Bake for 15 minutes at 400° F., then turn heat down to 325° F. and bake 25 minutes longer. Slide loaves onto a rack to cool. Makes 2 loaves, about 1 1/2 pounds each.

UNYEASTED WHOLE-WHEAT BREAD

An ancient, primitive way of making bread. During the waiting period a slight natural fermentation takes place which partly leavens the bread. You need not wait the full 24 hours, some people wait as few as 2 hours, but the longer you wait the lighter the bread.

> 3 cups whole-wheat
> flour
>
> 1 1/4 teaspoons salt
> 1 3/4 cups boiling water.

Put flour and salt in a bowl. With a wooden spoon stir in the boiling water. When well mixed, turn the dough onto a floured board. As soon as dough is cool enough to handle, knead it until smooth and silky, 3 to 5 minutes. Cut dough in half, knead each piece briefly. Turn over, so the smooth side is up, and with slightly cupped hands turn dough round and round to form a small round loaf. Set the two loaves on a lightly oiled baking sheet. Envelop the entire tray in plastic or cover each loaf with a bowl. Leave at room temperature for 24 hours. The loaves will hardly swell at all. Bake for 1 1/2 hours at 350° F. Loaves will remain almost exactly the same size. Slide loaves onto a rack to cool. Makes two tiny loaves about 3/4 pound each.

‡ COTTAGE CHEESE DILL BREAD

Serve with butter, cheese, or appetizer spreads. Delicious toasted or un-toasted with salads and soups.

> 1 cup creamed cottage
>   cheese, large or
>   small curd
> 1/4 cup water
> 1 tablespoon honey
> 1 envelope or 1
>   tablespoon dry yeast
> 1 tablespoon butter or
>   oil
>
> 1 egg
> 1 tablespoon minced
>   onion
> 2 tablespoons dried
>   dillweed
> 1 teaspoon salt
> About 2 1/2 cups
>   whole-wheat flour

In a 3-quart sauce pan, stir cottage cheese, water and honey over a low heat just until lukewarm. Remove from heat, stir in yeast. Let stand 5 minutes. Stir in butter or oil, the egg and remaining ingredients. When dough gets too stiff to stir, switch to using one hand instead. Add more whole-wheat flour if necessary to make a stiff dough that comes away from the side of the pan. Turn dough onto a floured board. Knead until smooth and silky, 3 to 5 minutes. As you knead, work in more flour if dough is still very sticky. Put dough, smooth side up, back in sauce pan. Cover with a damp cloth or with plastic. Let rise until double in bulk, about 1 hour. Turn dough back onto floured board and knead again briefly. Shape into one round loaf. Set on a baking sheet which has been lightly sprinkled with corn meal. Cover as before and let rise again until doubled. Bake for 45 minutes at 350° F. Cool on rack. Cool thoroughly before slicing. Makes 1 loaf, 1 pound 6 ounces. Keep in refrigerator.

‡ CHESTNUT FILBERT APPLE BREAD

A nutty, sweet, festive bread. Buy chestnut flour from an Italian or Middle Eastern grocery, or try a natural food store.

2 cups very warm water	1 teaspoon salt
1 envelope or 1 tablespoon dry yeast	About 3 cups whole-wheat flour
1 tablespoon honey	1/2 cup filberts, chopped
1/2 cup raisins	1 cup diced unpeeled dessert apple, like
1 cup chestnut flour	Golden Delicious

In a large bowl, mix the water, yeast, honey and raisins with a wooden spoon. Let stand 5 minutes. Meanwhile add remaining ingredients, except filberts and apple, to the bowl in order given, but don't stir them in until the 5 minutes are up. Now stir the mixture with the wooden spoon. As soon as it is too stiff to stir, switch to using one hand instead. Add more whole-wheat and chestnut flour if necessary, to make a stiff dough that comes away from the side of the bowl. Turn dough out onto a well-floured board. Knead until smooth and silky, 3 to 5 minutes. As you knead, work in more whole-wheat flour if dough is still very sticky. Put dough, smooth side up, back in bowl. Cover with a damp cloth or with plastic. Let rise until double in bulk, about 1 hour. Turn dough back onto floured board and knead again briefly. Cut up the apple, into approximately 1/4-inch pieces, and work into dough with the chopped filberts. Shape into one round loaf and set on a greased baking sheet. Cover as before and let rise again until doubled. Bake for 55 minutes at 350° F. A few of the raisins on the outside will scorch but don't worry. Slide loaf onto a rack to cool. Makes 1 loaf, about 2 1/2 pounds.

RAISIN OATMEAL STICKY BREAD

Dense and chewy, somewhere between a sweet bread and a not-very-sweet fruit cake. Flecks of oatmeal are visible in the finished loaf. This bread keeps and keeps, frozen or refrigerated.

1 envelope or 1 tablespoon dry yeast	*1 cup rolled oats, wheat flakes or barley flakes*
1/4 cup honey	*1 cup rye flour*
1/4 cup warm water	*1 teaspoon salt*
1/2 cup molasses	*1 cup raisins*
1 cup buttermilk	*1/2 cup coarsely chopped walnuts*
1 cup unbleached white flour	

Mix the yeast, honey and water in a 3-quart pan. Let stand 2 minutes. Mix in the molasses and buttermilk and stir over a low heat until the mixture is warm—about body temperature. Remove pan from heat. Dump in all remaining ingredients then stir them in. The batter will be thick, but beat it hard for about 50 strokes. Pour into a lightly buttered 8 x 4 x 2 -inch loaf pan. Let stand 30 minutes in a warm room. Loaf will not rise. Put pan into a cold oven; turn oven on and set to 300° F. Bake for 1 hour and 20 minutes. Turn heat up to 350° F. and bake 10 minutes longer. Turn out onto a rack to cool. If possible leave for a day before cutting. Serve in thin slices. Makes 1 heavy loaf, about 2 pounds. 1 cup cut-up pitted dates can replace raisins.

‡ OATCAKES

In Scotland, where my mother and this recipe come from, oil is rarely used for cooking. Instead, flavorful beef, pork or chicken drippings are used. Here we suggest oil, but if you're not overly cholesterol-conscious, try the drippings. In Scotland, an iron griddle, called a girdle, is standard equipment, and was used originally over an open fire.

1 1/2 **cups steel-cut oatmeal**	***About 1/4 cup whole wheat flour; or about 1/2 cup oat flour***
1 **tablespoon oil**	
3/4 **teaspoon salt**	
3/4 **cup hot water**	

In a bowl, mix oatmeal, oil and salt. Mix in hot water. Let stand 5 to 10 minutes—or longer if you wish. Mix in whole-wheat or oat flour, first with a spoon, and when the dough gets really stiff, with the fingers of one hand. Add more whole-wheat or oat flour if needed to make a stiff dough. Cut dough in half and press each piece firmly into a ball. Put one ball at a time between two sheets of wax paper and, with a rolling pin, roll out to about 12-inches in diameter; peel off top paper. Flip dough over onto ungreased cookie sheet, peel off remaining paper and cut dough into 8 wedges. Bake for 20 minutes at 350° F. Or cook wedges in unoiled iron skillet or iron griddle for about 10 minutes each side over medium heat; turn once only. If oatcakes start to curl on griddle, set a heavy pie plate on them to keep them flat. Serve oatcakes warm or cold with butter, miso spread, honey, or cheese. Serves 4 or less.

If you wish, make a double quantity of dough. Bake half as above, to use right away. Roll out rest of dough, cut in wedges, then wrap well and freeze on a flat plate. When needed, bake without thawing, and allow about 5 minutes extra cooking time.

ARMENIAN SESAME CRISPBREAD

*1 cup whole-wheat or
unbleached white
flour*
1/8 teaspoon salt
*2 teaspoons oil or
canned sesame
tahini*

*1/3 cup milk, or
buttermilk*
*Unhulled sesame seeds
(optional)*

Put flour and salt into a bowl. Drizzle oil over flour. Rub oil into flour by rubbing it between the palms of your hand; this takes about 1 minute. Pour milk into flour. With the fingers of one hand, mix milk into flour to make a dough. Put dough on a board. Either knead it for 5 minutes (difficult, because it's such a small piece of dough) or beat the dough aggressively for 5 minutes with a rolling pin; dough will gradually become quite smooth and silky. Cover or wrap dough, and leave at room temperature for 30 minutes. During this time the dough will relax. (If more convenient, refrigerate for 2 to 3 hours.) Cut dough into 4 pieces. Knead each piece briefly into a round, then put smooth side up on an unfloured board. With a rolling pin, roll out to 4 inches diameter. Sprinkle top with sesame seeds then continue rolling until dough is 7 to 8 inches in diameter. Put the flatbreads on a baking sheet. Bake in 400° F. oven for 10 to 12 minutes. Serve right away or later.

Variation: Sprinkle with grated cheese just before baking.

If you wish, make double or triple the quantity of dough and roll out and freeze some between sheets of wax paper or plastic wrap. Wrap stack of dough carefully, and place on something flat so it doesn't break. When needed, unwrap and bake as directed.

‡ CORN PONE

These corn pones are dense and chewy. Make them thinner and they'll be harder, crisper. Try different thickness to find which you like best.

> 3 cups stone ground whole yellow corn meal
> 3 tablespoons soy flour, sifted if lumpy
>
> 1 teaspoon salt
> 1 cup boiling water
> 1/4 cup corn oil or soft butter

In a bowl, mix corn meal, soy flour, and salt. Add boiling water and mix with a wooden spoon. Mix in oil and a little more water if any dry corn meal remains. Leave to cool, from 10 minutes to an hour—whichever is most convenient. Put the dough onto a lightly oiled baking sheet in quarter-cupfuls. (Use a quarter-cup measure, it's the quickest and most efficient way to divide the dough.) Then take a fork, dip it in water and flatten the pones slightly; they should be about 1/2-inch thick. Bake at 325° F. for 40 minutes. Serve hot or cold for breakfast or anytime. Makes 12.

If you like, make double the quantity of dough. Bake when you can and cool thoroughly. Wrap and freeze. When needed, corn pones thaw in about 10 minutes.

Yogurt

There are three good reasons for making your own yogurt: it tastes better than many commercial yogurts; it is free of added sugar, thickeners and preservatives, and the price is right.

Yogurt is milk into which specific bacteria are put. Given the desired warmth and conditions, the bacteria multiply; their action thickens the milk, changes the flavor, and produces the delicious food known as yogurt. Most manufacturers choose two bacteria from among these three: lactobacillus bulgaricus, lactobacillus acidophilus and streptococcus thermophilus.

To obtain the desired bacteria for making yogurt at home, you can buy a container of plain, regular commercial yogurt. Or, for a price, you can buy dried yogurt cultures.

Making yogurt is simple, once you have solved the basic problem: how to keep the innoculated milk at approximately 105 to 115° F. for at least 4 to 6 hours. One of the simplest ways is to wrap a heating pad set at a medium heat around the container of warmed milk, and fasten it with rubber bands.

Other ways are to:

1. Pour the warm milk into a clean, warm, vacuum (thermos) bottle.

2. Put a 15 watt light bulb inside an insulated container. Put the container of warm milk inside the insulated container. The heat from the light bulb will keep it warm.

3. Wrap the container of milk in an insulating layer of blankets and newspapers.

4. Use one of the commercial yogurt makers available, preferably not one with plastic containers as they tend to impart an unpleasant flavor to the yogurt.

TO MAKE YOGURT

Heat 1 to 2 quarts of milk just to boiling point. Pour into a straight-sided glass jar or properly glazed crockery container. Let cool. When between 110 to 115° F. stir in the yogurt cultures, or 1/3 to 2/3 cup fresh plain commercial yogurt. Cover the container and keep warm, by one of the methods described above, for 4 to 6 hours. (A thermometer takes the guesswork out of yogurt making.) Do not shake or disturb the milk. Test a spoonful after 3 hours. Uusally, yogurt is thick after 3 hours, but needs to incubate 2 to 4 hours longer to develope a good, tangy flavor. When ready, chill until needed. Save enough yogurt from each batch to culture the next one. Yogurt will keep a week or two. If the whey, a clear liquid, separates from the curd, simply stir it back in. Yogurt can be made with whole or skim milk, or skim with extra nonfat dry milk added. Whole milk tastes best.

Eat yogurt with fruit or vegetables or just by itself. It makes an excellent salad dressing, especially for sliced cucumbers. Yogurt is used in several recipes in this book; remember, however, that the desirable bacteria are killed off when heated above 120° F.

Nut Butters

RAW PEANUT BUTTER

Peanut butter is a snap to make with an electric blender and can be healthily free from the sugar and hydrogenated oil found in most supermarket kinds.

1 pound shelled raw peanuts, with or without skins	*Soybean or safflower oil* *Salt*

Put 1 cup of peanuts, 1 tablespoon oil, and 1/2 teaspoon salt in an electric blender. Whir until a smooth paste, then gradually drop in another cup of peanuts. If you think your blender can cope, continue to add remaining peanuts along with 1/2 teaspoon more salt, and, if mixture gets very stiff, another tablespoon of oil. Alternatively, if blender seems to balk, scoop out the first batch and start over with remaining peanuts. Store in refrigerator to prevent oil separation. Makes 1 3/4 cups.

Roasted Peanut Butter: Bake raw peanuts in a roasting pan in a 300° F. oven, 15 to 20 minutes, or until a pale brown. Shake pan once or twice. Cool nuts. Then make butter as above, but put 2 tablespoons of oil in the blender to begin with.

OTHER NUT BUTTERS AND SEED BUTTERS

You can make delicious nut butters out of almonds, cashews, pecans, and walnuts, separately or mixed. For seed butters, use sunflower or sesame seeds; or mix seeds and nuts. To make, put 1 tablespoon oil in electric blender with 1/4 teaspoon salt and 1/2 cup of the chosen nut or seed. Turn on machine for a few seconds, then stop and push mixture down. Repeat two or three times. Here are three good combinations, each of which makes about 1/2 cup.

Sesame Almond Butter: 1/3 cup unhulled sesame seeds, 1/3 cup almonds, 4 tablespoons oil, 1/4 teaspoon salt.

Cashew Walnut Butter: 1/2 cup raw cashew nuts, 1/2 cup walnuts, 3 tablespoons oil, 1/8 teaspoon salt.

Peanut Almond Butter: 1/3 cup raw peanuts, 1/3 cup raw almonds, 2 tablespoons oil, 1/8 teaspoon salt.

SESAME HONEY PEANUT SPREAD

1 tablespoon sesame seeds, toasted or raw

1/2 cup peanut butter
1 tablespoon honey

If seeds are not toasted, put in a small deep pan, shake over medium high heat for 2 to 3 minutes. When they start flying out of the pan, and crumble between the fingers, seeds are ready. Put in a bowl and crush slightly with back of a wooden spoon. (Or use a mortar and pestle, or a suribachi.) Do not break up all the seeds. Mix with the peanut butter and the honey. Makes 1/2 cup.

Other Homemade Healthy Things

SPROUTED SEEDS AND GRAINS

Sprouts are young, newly germinated seeds, eaten at the tender age of 4 to 5 days. They are frequently touted as being miraculously endowed with vitamins and minerals, especially vitamin C. Although they do contain more of some vitamins than the original seeds, a glance at the USDA food composition charts shows that it is certainly not a miraculous amount, especially when compared with high-in-C foods such as strawberries and green peppers.

Sprouts are fun to grow, especially in a city or in the wintertime. Besides, who'd want to sit down to eat a bowl of dry alfalfa seeds? But when those seeds are sprouted and turn into tender, pale green shoots, they are perfectly delicious.

Although you can sprout all kinds of whole seeds, the most useful ones are wheat, alfalfa, and mung beans. Buy seeds that are specifically intended for sprouting, and not for planting, so as to avoid any that have been treated with agricultural chemicals.

TO SPROUT

No special equipment is needed, just a wide-mouthed glass jar and some netting (cheesecloth, nylon net, a piece of old hose) to tie over the top.

Put the seeds in a jar, rinse with cold water, then cover with fresh cold water. Leave until well swollen, 8 to 12 hours. Fasten a piece of net over top of jar with a rubber band or piece of twine. Pour off water, rinse seeds with fresh cold water and leave upside down for a minute or two to drain thoroughly. Shake jar so seeds don't all stay in a clump. Put jar in a dark place—such as a kitchen cupboard. Then each morning and evening, (and once during the day, too, if you're there) rinse seeds with fresh cold water and drain well. Within a day and a half you will see activity. The seeds will burst their jackets and a tiny shoot emerge from each one.

Sprouting times differ slightly according to the atmosphere—in a warm place, seeds sprout faster. It's important to keep them moist, but if left in a puddle of water, they will ferment. Highly chlorinated water is said to sometimes prevent sprouting.

Wheat sprouts are ready when the sprout is as long as the kernel, in 2 to 3 days. Stop rinsing, and refrigerate until ready to use. Wheat sprouts are delicious in sprouted wheat bread (see recipe); they can be added to a salad, or cooked for 1 minute in a soup. One cup wheat kernels yields 3 cups sprouts.

Mung bean sprouts are ready when they are 1 to 1 1/2 inches long, about 4 days. They taste better with the green jackets washed away: put the sprouts in a colander set in a large bowl. Fill bowl with water, then dunk colander up and down many times. Most of the jackets will flow out through the holes. Cook mung bean sprouts Chinese style for a few seconds only. They can be used alone, or added to other vegetables. One-half cup mung beans yields 4 cups sprouts.

Alfalfa, the tiniest seeds, take the longest time to reach harvest age. After about 3 days, when the shoots are 1 1/2 to 2 inches long, leave the jar of sprouts in daylight between rinsings—perhaps on a sunny windowsill. They are ready to eat when the tiny leaves are bright green and can then be kept for several days in the refrigerator. Alfalfa sprouts are eaten raw; add them to a mixed green salad, use instead of lettuce in a sandwich. One fourth cup alfalfa seeds yield 6 cups sprouts.

YOGURT CHEESE (Lebayeen)

1 quart yogurt

Line a 1 1/2- to 2-quart bowl with two layers of cheesecloth; use a large enough piece so cheesecloth hangs over edge of bowl. Pour yogurt into cheesecloth, gather up cheesecloth and tie it with a long piece of twine. Hang up to drain, with a bowl beneath to catch the whey. Leave for 4 hours, or up to 12. Unwrap cheesecloth and spoon out cheese. Chill until needed. Chill the whey, then drink it as a refreshing beverage. Yields about 1 1/2 to 2 cups yogurt cheese, and about the same amount of whey.

To Use Yogurt Cheese: Eat as is—the flavor is sharp and tangy. Or mix 1/2 cup lebayeen with 1/4 teaspoon dried mint, 1 teaspoon olive oil, and a pinch of salt; serve with bread and olives for breakfast as they do in Syria and Israel. (Green or black olives imported from Greece are best.) Sometimes lebayeen is served in a bowl with a thin layer of olive oil poured over the top, and scallions or chives instead of mint.

Lebayeen Topping: Mix 1/2 cup yogurt cheese with about 1 tablespoon honey. Serve as topping, or as a dipping sauce for fresh fruit.

GOMASIO

From the macrobiotic diet regime comes this seasoned salt. It's delicious on avocado slices, tomatoes, salads, and in vegetable soups. In spite of the small proportion of salt, gomasio tastes distinctly salty, so if you're trying to cut down the amount of salt the family adds to food, put this seasoning on the table as an alternative.

1/2 cup unhulled sesame seeds	*1 teaspoon kosher, sea, or regular salt*

Put seeds into a small, deep pan. Shake or stir over medium heat for 2 to 3 minutes to roast. When done, seeds will start shooting out of pan, be very slightly browned, smell roasted, and crumble easily in the fingers. Remove from heat and put into electric blender. Put salt in pan, shake over medium heat for a minute or two. Set aside. Whir seeds in blender for a few seconds. Then add salt and blend again until about 80 percent of the seeds are crushed. Keep gomasio in a screwtop jar. Serve in a shaker with large holes, or in a bowl. Gomasio keeps well. Makes about 1/2 cup. (If you don't have a blender, use a mortar, or suribachi.)

MISO SPREAD

Macrobiotic dieters use miso spread instead of butter, but you don't have to be macrobiotic to enjoy its rich, meaty flavor. Try it with light miso first, as the dark is quite strong. Buy the paste in health and oriental food stores. After opening, it will keep forever in the refrigerator. The spread keeps for weeks, too.

1 tablespoon oil	*4 tablespoons water*
1/2 cup finely chopped onion	*2 tablespoons light or dark miso paste*
1/2 cup tahini (canned sesame paste)	

Warm the oil in a 1 1/2-quart pan. Stir in onion and let cook, covered, over medium heat for about 2 minutes. Remove lid from pan and let onions brown slowly, 3 to 4 minutes longer. Stir often. Now stir in the tahini and stir over medium heat for 3 to 5 minutes. Have the water handy, and as soon as the tahini is a milky coffee color, stir in the water, 1 tablespoon at a time. Then stir in the miso, 1 tablespoon at a time. Stir over heat 2 minutes longer. Serve cold as a dip or as a spread for bread. Makes almost 1 cup.

STOCK OR BROTH

Stock in its simplest form is made by simmering bones and/or vegetables and seasonings in water. That's all.

Buy 2 to 3 pounds of beef bones, put them in a pan, cover with cold water, bring slowly to a boil and then let simmer, covered for 3 hours. Strain out the bones; the liquid is your stock. Chill the stock if you can, then skim off any fat before using. If you have a few slices of onion, leek, carrot, or celery around, add them to the pot, too. A tiny amount of turnip is also fine. Parsley stems help. Cut vegetables up in small pieces so their flavor seeps out. For seasoning, add if you like 6 to 8 peppercorns, a small bay leaf, a tiny pinch of thyme, or small pieces of blade mace. Cabbage, broccoli, cauliflower, spinach, squash, potatoes, beets and sweet potatoes are not good for stockmaking.

Make *chicken stock* the same way as above, using backbones; simmer no more than 2 hours.

Veal bones don't give much flavor to stock, but they can make it jell when cold. Usually, veal bones are mixed with beef bones.

Fish stock is a good way to get the last out of a fish. Use raw bones and heads from nonoily fish (flounder, cod, etc.). Simmer 12 to 20 minutes. After that time a bitter flavor starts to develop. Any vegetables used can be given a headstart of 20 to 30 minutes.

Vegetable stock is made by simmering the suggested vegetables in water with seasonings. Vegetable stock can also be water left over from cooking vegetables. To make a weak stock stronger, simmer it uncovered until some of the water has evaporated. Try to avoid doing this as extended cooking time and fast boiling destroy a stock's fresh flavor.

9

❦

Little Things Can Mean a Lot

Americans have become a nation of habitual snackers, bolting down everything from fried orange-colored squiggles to pink cupcakes filled with sugar and shortening, and millions of potato chips dunked in oceans of soup mix and sour cream. The calories are high, the nutritional contribution comparatively low.

There's nothing wrong with snacking, it's what we snack on. Many people are happier and healthier eating small amounts frequently. Fast-growing, energetic teenagers often need snacks between meals to help supply them with enough calories in a day. If you want to switch to the healthy-snack track, here are a few thoughts.

First, gradually cut down and out all deep-fried snack items such as potato chips, corn chips and the aforementioned orange squiggles. Not only are their calorie and fat contents high (around 40 percent fat) but they are cooked in oils that are heated to high temperatures for long periods which may actually produce hazardous substances in the fat.

Second, check the ingredient listing on boxes of cookies, crackers and pretzels you buy. Avoid all those where the major ingredients (those listed first on the label) are sugar, shortening and white flour—see shopping guide for good brand names.

Third, gradually wean the family away from sodas, dietetic or not, and all drink mixes that consist of sugar and artificial flavors and colors. Cut down, too, on candy and chewing gum.

Fourth, and most important of all—offer nutritious, good tasting alternatives: When next your candy jar is empty, fill it with raw shelled nuts or seeds such as almonds, peanuts, pumpkin seeds, or sunflower seeds. If you like roasted nuts, toast them yourself with a little fresh oil or butter in a skillet, or alternatively bake the nuts in a 350° F. oven until brown. Then toss, if you wish, with a tiny amount of oil, or butter, and salt.

Dried fruits such as dates, figs, raisins and prunes are delicious, nutritious, and satisfy a craving for something sweet. However, they do stick to the teeth as tightly as candy. Teach children to clean their teeth or at least to eat an apple, a piece of crunchy celery, or even a nut or two after eating sweet, sticky foods. Alternatively they can always rinse their mouths out thoroughly with water.

If I had children hooked on sodas I think I would quietly investigate the possibility of renting a water cooler. Part of the fascination of sodas is the sophisticated opening of cans and bottles. A water cooler is impressive, and might just divert their attention to plain water or to fruit juices diluted with water. To get that carbonated feeling, use plain club soda, alone, or mixed with fruit juice.

If you have an abundant supply of fruits and vegetables you may want to consider a juicer. This is a machine that liquifies carrots, apples, celery, cabbage, etc. into juice, removing just the cellulose. The juices can be spectacularly delicious; however, a juicer is expensive and should only be considered if it will really be put to use and not gather dust on the kitchen shelf.

Menu-Maker's Guide

Goodies, sweet or salty, to munch on:

‡ Crunchy Soybeans
‡ Survival Snack
  Toasted Coconut
‡ Onion Thins
‡ Whole-Wheat Cheese Crisps

Whole-Wheat Cookie-Crackers
Parkin

Dips, Spreads, and Sandwiches:

‡ Black Bean Dip
‡ Tapenade (tuna or mackerel with capers)
‡ Skordalia (garlic-potato dip)
  Baba Ghannou (eggplant dip with sesame)
  Soybean Spread
  Avocado Yogurt Dip
  Spinach Yogurt Dip
  Bread and Cheese
  Melted Cheese
‡ Avocado, Bacon, Tomato and Alfalfa Sprout Sandwich
  Muenster and Alfalfa Sprout Sandwich
‡ Pumpkin Seed and Raisin Sandwich

Beverages:

‡ Almond Milk (but no milk)
  Golden Milk
  Carob Milk
‡ Persian Yogurt Drink
  Milk, Banana, and Molasses
  Apricot Milk
‡ Yogurt Whip
‡ Beet and Buttermilk Drink
‡ Orange and Strawberry Juice
  Strawberry Pineapple Juice
‡ Cranberry Pineapple Juice
  Orange Juice and Milk
  Lemonade
  Pineapple and Watercress Drink

Two Specials:

  Ginger Tea
‡ Sekanjabin

For more snack ideas see cookies and candies, yogurt, miso spread, cold cereals, grains and falafel.

‡ CRUNCHY SOY BEANS

1 cup soybeans	*About 2 teaspoons oil*
3 cups water	*About 1/4 teaspoon salt*

Soak soybeans in water in refrigerator for 8 to 24 hours. Tip soybeans into a strainer, rinse under the cold faucet and let drain for 5 minutes. Spread out in a single layer in a roasting pan then bake for 1 hour in a 350° F. oven. Shake 4 or 5 times during that period and watch carefully during the last 15 minutes. Beans will darken and get crunchy, but don't let them scorch. Remove pan from oven, let cool a little, then sprinkle oil and salt over beans. Mix thoroughly between palms of your hands until beans are coated with oil and salt. Cool and store in an airtight container. Makes about 1 1/2 cups.

‡ SURVIVAL SNACK

The backpackers favorite, and great to take in airplane or automobile.

Raisins or currants	*Raw, unroasted, shelled*
Sunflower or pumpkin	*nuts—almonds, filberts,*
kernels	*peanuts or cashews*

Take a paper or plastic bag. Put in dried fruit, nuts and seeds in any proportion or quantity you like. Try: 1/4 cup each raisins, sunflower seeds, pumpkin seeds and almonds. *Or:* 1 cup each raw peanuts and currants. *Or:* 1/4 cup raisins, 1/4 cup raw peanuts, 1/4 cup sunflower seeds. Almost anything works; mix a mouthful first and sample.

TOASTED COCONUT

Eat with drinks, or use to top salads and desserts.

> *1 coconut (check to   Salt (optional)*
> *see shell is*
> *uncracked)*

Pierce two soft "eyes" of coconut with a skewer or screwdriver and drain out liquid (drink it if you wish). Put coconut on a shelf in oven and bake for 1 hour at 250° F. If shell hasn't then cracked open by itself, bang with a hammer or drop on a concrete floor. Lift out meat which will have shrunk from shell. Cut in long strips with a vegetable peeler; each strip will have a thin edge of brown skin. Let strips fall on a baking sheet or into a roasting pan. Sprinkle lightly with salt. Bake for 20 to 25 minutes at 325° F. Move strips around once or twice so they brown evenly and do not scorch. When done, coconut will be a light brown color. Store in an airtight container.

‡ ONION THINS

Serve with drinks, or with soup or salad.

> *1 tablespoon oil   1 tablespoon soy flour,*
> *1/3 cup minced onion   if available*
> *1/4 cup canned sesame   2 tablespoons soy*
> *tahini   sauce*
> *1 cup rolled oats,   1/2 cup whole-wheat*
> *whirred in blender   flour*
> *to break up   1/4 cup milk*
> *1/2 teaspoon salt*

Warm oil in a 1- to 2-quart pan; stir in onion then cover and cook 4 minutes over low heat to soften. Stir in tahini. Turn heat up a little and keep stirring tahini-onion mixture until it is about 2 shades darker and smells roasted—about 2 minutes. Remove pan from heat. Immediately stir in oats. Then stir in salt, soy flour, soy sauce and whole-wheat flour. Lastly stir in milk. Dough will be stiff. Remove dough from pan, shape into a rectangle and place on a large cookie sheet. With a rolling pin roll out dough to a rectangle about 1/10th-inch thick; cut into 24 rectangles. Bake at 375° F. for about 10 minutes. Crackers should be crisp, but take care that they do not scorch. Cool before storing in an airtight container. Makes 24.

‡ WHOLE-WHEAT CHEESE CRISPS

Satisfying for snacks, as an appetizer, or with soup, these quick-to-make crisps are rather fragile and should be eaten the day they are baked.

1 cup grated cheddar cheese (about 3 ounces)
3/4 cup whole-wheat pastry flour

4 tablespoons oil or butter
1/4 teaspoon salt

Put all ingredients in a bowl. With one hand, mix ingredients, then press together to form one lump of dough. Put dough on a cookie sheet. Form into rectangle. Roll out with rolling pin to a 10 x 7 inch rectangle. Cut into 20 small rectangles. Bake at 350° F., for 20 minutes. Go over the knife marks if necessary to separate pieces, then slide onto a rack to cool. Makes 20 crisps.

WHOLE-WHEAT COOKIE-CRACKERS

Slightly sweet, cookie **cum** *crackers, good for a snack with cheese or a glass of milk.*

2/3 cup oat flour, or 3/4 cup rolled oats
1 1/2 cups whole-wheat flour
1/2 teaspoon salt

6 tablespoons butter or oil (or a mixture)
1 tablespoon honey
Milk, about 2 tablespoons

If using rolled oats, first whir them in an electric blender until as like "flour" as possible. Put oat flour, whole-wheat flour and salt in a bowl. Add butter, cut into pieces, or drizzle oil over. Then drizzle honey over. Now rub butter (or oil) into flour mixture by scooping up mixture in each hand and rubbing it between thumb and fingers. Work quickly. Keep scooping up and rubbing fat and flour together until mixture looks crumbly and damp. Add 2 tablespoons of milk to bowl; mix in with fingers of one hand. Add more milk if needed, until dough holds together in a ball when pressed. Put dough onto a cookie sheet; shape into a disk. Roll out until about 1/4 inch thick, 10 inches in diameter; prick all over with a fork, cut into 16 wedges. Bake at 350° F., 25 minutes. Slide onto rack to cool. Makes 16.

PARKIN

Wrap and keep for a day or two before cutting. Serve with coffee, or with cheese for lunch or a snack. Good "traveling" food.

2 1/4 **cups rolled oats**	1/4 **teaspoon salt**
4 **tablespoons butter**	1/16 **teaspoon ground**
3/4 **cup molasses,**	**cloves**
preferably not	1 **egg**
blackstrap	1 1/2 **cups whole-wheat**
1/4 **teaspoon ground**	**flour**
ginger	

Put oats in electric blender and whir until well broken up—but not too powdery. Warm butter and molasses together in a pan until butter is melted. Remove from heat, stir in ground-up oats, ginger, salt, cloves and egg. Then stir in whole-wheat flour. Mixture will be stiff. Spread evenly into a lightly oiled 8-inch square baking pan. Bake at 350° F. for about 30 minutes; Parkin will rise very little. Turn onto a rack to cool. Cut into squares before serving. Makes 16 squares.

Dips, Spreads and Sandwiches

Dipping crisp things into creamy dips has become part of the American way of life. Perhaps many people think of dips as an American invention but a glance at these recipes shows that dipping has been going on for centuries in Greece (Skordalia), the Mediterranean (Tapenade), and the Middle Eastern countries (Baba Ghannou).

Too many dips are high in sour cream and calories; dippers of potato chips or corn chips only pile the calories on. The recipes here are mainly based on vegetables, yogurt or fish. Serve them with raw vegetable sticks (carrot, celery, green pepper, rutabagas, cauliflower sprigs, zucchini slices, mushrooms), plain breads or flat breads such as Armenian Sesame Crispbread (see page oo).

‡ BLACK BEAN DIP

If you wish, add chopped canned green chili peppers or a little lemon juice to this dip. I like it just the way it is, but some people think it a little bland. Leftovers taste good for breakfast.

1 1/4 cups dried black beans	*1/2 cup sour cream or yogurt, or 1/4 cup of each*
1-inch bay leaf	
1 teaspoon salt	

Soak beans for 8 to 24 hours in 3 cups cold water in refrigerator. Bring to boil in soaking water, add bay leaf and salt. Simmer covered until tender, 1 to 1 1/2 hours; little water should remain. Put yogurt or sour cream in electric blender. Add half the beans and whir smooth. Add remaining beans and whir again but don't let mixture get too smooth. Stop blender and push beans down if necessary. If too stiff, add a little of cooking liquid. Serve chilled or at room temperature. Makes just over 2 cups.

‡ TAPENADE—A Mediterranean dip

This piquant spread keeps about 2 weeks in the refrigerator. Serve with halved hard-cooked eggs on a small plate, or as a dip with raw vegetables. Good with a plain bread.

1/4 cup oil, olive is best
1/2 teaspoon lemon
   juice
3 tablespoons capers,
   rinsed and drained
1 can (4 3/8 ounces)
   mackerel fillets; or
   1 can (3 1/2

ounces) tuna,
   drained
1 can (2 ounces) flat
   anchovy fillets,
   drained
1 can (3 1/2 ounces)
   ripe black olives,
   drained

Put oil, lemon juice, capers, mackerel (or tuna) and anchovies in electric blender. If olives have pits in, remove them with your fingers. Add olives to blender. Blend at low speed until a fairly smooth mixture is obtained. Stop machine two or three times to push ingredients down. Serve at once or chill. Makes about 1 cup.

‡ SKORDALIA

*If you don't like garlic—although garlic is what Skordalia is all about— add plenty chopped fresh chives to the potato mixture **after** blending.*

Serve this thick creamy spread on a small plate as an appetizer. In Greece where this dish comes from, it is served with slices of cooked beet.

1 pound baking
   potatoes
3/4 cup oil, olive is best
3 tablespoons cider
   vinegar

2 to 3 teaspoons
   minced garlic
1/2 teaspoon salt

Put unpeeled potatoes on a steamer rack over 1-inch of boiling water in a pan. Cover tightly and cook until tender, 20 to 25 minutes. When cool enough to handle, peel potatoes and break up into small pieces. Put 1/4 cup oil, 2 tablespoons vinegar, 2 teaspoons garlic and the salt into an electric blender. Add about quarter of the potatoes and whir smooth. Stop machine, push down mixture, add 1/4 cup more oil and another quarter of the potatoes; whir again. Add and blend remaining oil and potatoes. Stop machine and taste mixture. Add more garlic or vinegar if you wish. Chill before serving. Makes about 2 cups.

BABA GHANNOU—Eggplant Appetizer

Serve with pita bread from a Middle Eastern store, sesame flat bread (page 000) or any plain bread. Some Middle Eastern cooks like to season the eggplant with finely chopped onion, vinegar, salt and fresh or dried mint instead of sesame paste, lemon juice and garlic.

1 eggplant, about 1 to 1 1/2 pounds	*About 2 tablespoons lemon juice*
2 tablespoons canned sesame tahini, or olive oil	*About 1 teaspoon chopped garlic*
	About 3/4 teaspoon salt

Wipe the eggplant, but don't do anything else to it. Put on rack under broiler and broil fairly close to the heat for 10 minutes. Turn eggplant over and broil about 10 minutes longer. Stick a knife or skewer into the eggplant to make sure it is tender in the middle. Cut off eggplant stem, then cut vegetable in half lengthwise. Leave on peel unless badly charred—the appetizer will have a more earthy flavor. If you prefer a light flavor, scrape flesh off peel. Put eggplant in an electric blender. Add remaining ingredients in quantities suggested and blend smooth. Then taste and add more lemon, garlic, or salt if you wish. Makes about 1 1/2 cups.

SOYBEAN SPREAD

If no blender is available, mash the beans thoroughly, or grind them in a suribachi.

1 cup dried soybeans,	*About 1/2 cup lemon juice*
or 2 cups cooked	*About 1/2 teaspoon salt*
soybeans	*About 1/2 teaspoon*
2 tablespoons olive oil	*minced garlic*

If using dried soybeans, soak them 8 to 12 hours in 2 1/2 cups of water in refrigerator. Bring to boil in soaking liquid; simmer covered until tender, about 2 hours. Put oil, lemon juice, salt, and garlic in electric blender; add about 1/2 cup cooked drained soybeans and blend smooth. Gradually add remaining soybeans. Stop machine, taste spread and add more seasoning if you wish. Chill before serving as dip for raw vegetables, or with bread as an appetizer. Makes about 2 cups.

AVOCADO YOGURT DIP

1 ripe avocado (about	*1 tablespoon thinly*
12 ounces)	*sliced chives or*
3/4 cup yogurt	*scallions*
1/4 teaspoon salt	

Peel avocado, cut in half and remove pit. Mash avocado on a plate until smooth. Mash in yogurt, salt and chives. Taste, add more salt if you wish. Makes about 1 3/4 cups.

SPINACH YOGURT DIP

Do not be tempted to make this in the blender unless you wish to have a rather unusually flavored spinach-yogurt soup!

2 tablespoons hulled sesame seeds, raw or toasted	1/4 cup finely sliced scallions
1 cup plain yogurt	1/4 teaspoon dry mustard
1/2 cup finely chopped fresh spinach	1/2 teaspoon salt
	Black pepper to taste

To toast raw seeds, put them in a small deep pan and shake slowly over medium heat for 3 to 4 minutes. When toasted, the seeds will start to pop and fly, smell toasted, and crumble between two fingers. Whir toasted seeds briefly in blender to break up, or grind them in a suribachi. Mix gently with remaining ingredients. Serve at once or chill. Makes about 1 cup. Serve with raw zucchini, radishes or mushrooms.

BREAD AND CHEESE

Bread and cheese, when both are good, make a satisfying lunch or snack anywhere at anytime. In the past few years, cheese shops have sprung up all over America, many carrying such an awesome selection of cheeses that it's hard to know where to start. Here are a few combinations good for lunch, supper or picnic fare.

Whole-wheat bread, Cheddar cheese, ripe tomatoes, and possibly a pickle
Taleggio cheese, whole-wheat bread, radishes
Pont l'Eveque cheese, celery
Kumminost cheese with sliced fresh cucumber and paprika
Edam cheese with rye bread and radishes
Gruyère cheese with pumpernickel bread

MELTED CHEESE

1 thick slice (2 ounces) Muenster or Monterey cheese	Few slices raw mushroom (optional)
Garlic (optional)	Raw vegetables and chunks of bread for dipping

Use a small oven-proof dish about the size of the cheese slice. Rub a cut garlic clove around bottom of baking dish—use garlic later for something else. Lay cheese in dish, put mushroom slices on top. Broil 2 to 3 minutes until just melted. Serve at once, with carrot sticks, green pepper sticks, and chunks of whole-wheat bread to dip into it. Serves 1.

Three Sandwiches

‡ *Avocado, Bacon, Tomato and Alfalfa Sprout Sandwich:* Spread soft, ripe avocado on two slices of toasted white or whole-wheat bread. Sprinkle with salt. Top one slice with about 4 strips of crisp cooked bacon, tomato slices and a little mound of alfalfa sprouts. Top with second slice of toast.

Muenster with Alfalfa Sprouts: Between slices of buttered whole-wheat bread put a mound of alfalfa sprouts and two slices of Meunster or Monterey cheese.

‡ *Pumpkin Seed and Raisin Sandwich:* Very rich, so use this amount of filling to make two sandwiches and serve them with cottage cheese and fresh fruit.

Whir 1/2 cup pumpkin kernels and 1/4 cup raisins in electric blender until well broken up. Tip into a bowl and mix in 1 tablespoon yogurt. Serve on whole-wheat bread. Makes 1/2 cup filling. Sunflower seeds combined with figs, or walnuts with raisins, make equally good sandwich fillings.

Beverages

‡ ALMOND MILK

1/2 cup shelled almonds	*1 cup boiling water*
(leave skins on)	*1 teaspoon honey*

Grind nuts in electric blender. Add boiling water and whir for about 30 seconds. Strain into a bowl. Press almonds with back of a spoon to extract as much liquid as possible. Stir in honey and drink from bowl, or transfer to a glass. Makes 3/4 cup. Try making "milk" with sunflower seeds or unhulled sesame seeds. Use leftover ground nuts in salads, in bread, or to top vegetables.

GOLDEN MILK

1/4 cup shelled almonds, *1 egg*
  (leave skins on) *1 tablespoon honey*
1/2 cup boiling water *1 cup very hot milk*

Put almonds in electric blender. Add boiling water, cover, and blend for one minute. Add egg and honey; whir again briefly. Pour in the milk, which should be just at boiling point to "cook" the egg white. Whir for a few seconds. Drink without straining. Makes 2 1/4 cups.

CAROB MILK

1 cup milk *1 1/2 tablespoons carob*
2 teaspoons honey *powder*
  Dash vanilla extract

Whir all together in electric blender. Makes 1 cup.

‡ PERSIAN YOGURT DRINK

Yogurt *1 teaspoon chopped*
1/4 teaspoon crumbled *fresh mint*
  dried mint, or *Cold water*

Half fill a tall glass with yogurt, stir in mint. Fill glass with water, stir again and drink.

MILK, BANANA, AND MOLASSES

1 cup milk
1 banana
1 tablespoon molasses

1 teaspoon instant coffee powder (optional)

Whir smooth in electric blender. Makes 1 1/2 cups.

APRICOT MILK

1 cup (2 ounces) unsulphured dried apricots

3 cups cold water
2 cups milk

For this drink, you can use the very hard, impossible-to-chew sun-dried apricots. Soak apricots 4 hours or longer in water. Whir smooth in electric blender. Gradually add cold milk. Makes 3 cups.

‡ YOGURT WHIP

1 cup yogurt
About 1/2 cup fresh fruit

About 1 teaspoon honey

Put yogurt and fruit in electric blender. Whir smooth. Taste. Add honey as desired and blend again. Makes about 1 1/4 cups. Good made with strawberries, blueberries, raspberries, peaches, fresh or soaked dried apricots.

‡ BEET AND BUTTERMILK DRINK

1/4 cup diced peeled   *1 cup buttermilk*
  raw beets   *Pinch salt*

Whir all together in electric blender. Tastes like borscht with sour cream. Makes 1 1/4 cups.

‡ ORANGE AND STRAWBERRY JUICE

1 cup orange juice   *1/4 cup nonfat dry milk*
1/4 cup sliced   *(optional)*
  strawberries
  (unsugared)

Whir smooth in electric blender. Makes 1 1/2 cups.

STRAWBERRY-PINEAPPLE JUICE

1 cup unsweetened   *1 teaspoon honey*
  pineapple juice
1/2 cup cut-up
  strawberries

Whir smooth in electric blender. Makes 1 1/3 cups.

‡ CRANBERRY-PINEAPPLE JUICE

2 cups unsweetened   *1/2 cup fresh or frozen*
  pineapplejuice   *cranberries*

Whir smooth in electric blender. Makes 2 1/3 cups.

ORANGE JUICE AND MILK

1/2 cup orange juice
1/2 cup milk

1/2 cup sliced
strawberries
(optional)

Stir the orange juice and milk together. Makes 1 cup. For the strawberry version, whir all together in electric blender. Makes 1 1/2 cups.

LEMONADE

1 1/2 cups water
1/4 cup honey

1/2 cup lemon juice

Mix all together. Makes 2 cups. Pour over ice cubes to serve.

PINEAPPLE AND WATERCRESS DRINK

1 cup unsweetened
pineapple juice
1/2 cup coarsely
chopped tightly
packed watercress

Whir together in electric blender. Makes 1 cup.

GINGER TEA

1/4 cup diced unpeeled
fresh ginger root
1/2 inch strip lemon
rind cut with a
vegetable peeler

1/2 cup boiling water
1/4 cup honey
1/4 cup lemon juice

Put ginger and lemon rind in electric blender. Add boiling water and whir well. Add honey and lemon juice. Whir briefly. Strain into a jar for storing. Makes about 1 cup. To serve, pour about 2 tablespoons into a cup of regular tea.

‡ SEKANJABIN

The Iranian equivalent of a Prohibition mint julep.

2 cups water	20 to 25 stalks of mint*
1 cup distilled white	1 1/2 cups honey
or cider vinegar	1/2 cup lemon juice

Heat water and vinegar in a pan; simmer, uncovered, for 10 minutes. Add mint and simmer 3 to 4 minutes longer, pressing mint down with a wooden spoon. Remove pan from heat. Stir in honey and lemon juice. Strain and pour into a bottle or jar for keeping. Makes about 3 1/2 cups. To serve, pour about 1/4 cup sekanjabin over ice cubes in a glass. Top up with water and stir.

*Recipe does not work with dried mint.

10

The Healthy Pantry

Using a wide variety of delicious, nutritious foods will make life more pleasurable and meal-planning simpler. To obtain them, shop in all the places you can: supermarket, farm market, butcher's shop, fish market, health food store, and stores that stock Chinese, Spanish or Middle Eastern groceries. The classified phone directory can be helpful as, for example, in locating Greek groceries in Boston. If you don't have access to the varied stores of a city, then shop by mail for whole grains, nuts and seeds. You will find a short list of sources at the end of this book.

The healthy pantry eschews dubious foods like liver pills and pollen. On the other hand it accomodates yogurt, wheat germ and molasses, but doesn't set them on a pedestal. Primarily, the healthy pantry is filled with fruits, vegetables, meats, fish, eggs, grains and dairy products, all carefully chosen for their nutritional values, and processed as little as possible. In each chapter you will find information that will help you to shop well.

Today, so many food products are polluted with additives that when trying to decide whether a certain product is really worth buying or not, you might want to judge it by the standards Organic Merchants, a group of food store owners, set for products they stock in their own stores. To eliminate food pollution (and, importantly, a lot of environmental pollution, too) at the manufacturing, processing and packaging levels, "no OM will sell any food containing artificial flavor, artificial color, monosodium glutamate, synthetic sugar substitute, synthetic salt substitute, synthetic preservatives, emulsifiers 'or other synthetic food chemicals, corn syrup, white sugar, bleached white flour, cottonseed products or hydrogenated fats." OM acknowledges that this doesn't help us eliminate food pollution from agricultural chemicals, but at least it's a start.

It's important to keep tuned in to what's going on in the world of government agencies in relation to food additives. Since this book was started, several presently permitted additives are coming under Food and Drug Administration scrutiny, and the United States Department of Agriculture is supporting some research to develop ways of controlling pests other than toxic sprays. There's hope.

A brief shopping guide follows. It is designed to help you select the most delicious and nutritious foods for your family. It would be difficult to use all the grain products available, so the ones I find most useful and enjoyable are italicized; one grain may be available in many forms, such as whole, hulled, ground into flour or cracked.

Item	*Choose From*	*Not Recommended*
BACON	High in fat, so use as a garnish, rather than a protein food. Canadian bacon is better protein buy.	
BARLEY	*Natural brown.* Hulled. *Barley flour.*	
BEVERAGES	Fresh, frozen, or canned fruit and vegetable juices. Water. Club soda.	Punches, -ades, juice "drinks," nectars, powdered drink mixes. Sodas, whether sugar- free or not.
BREAKFAST CEREALS	Preferably whole grain, for hot or cold use.	Cereals with sugar, cocoa, marshmallows, artificial coloring, fruit flavorings.

BUCKWHEAT	Groats (kasha). Flour.	
BULGUR	Parched wheat; any grind.	
BUTTERMILK	Cultured, or if you can find it, the real thing.	
CANNED FRUIT	Packed in water or fruit juice. Use to add variety to diet between seasons.	Packed in syrup or with the artificial sweeteners now in use.
CANNED VEGETABLES	Fresh or frozen are generally better, but okay to add variety to diet.	
CAROB	Powdered St. John's bread. Used as cocoa-chocolate substitute.	
CHEESE	Natural, unprocessed cheeses, without preservatives or coloring. Made from pasteurized milk.	
COCONUT	Fresh, check shell is uncracked.	
COOKIES	Made with whole grains or flours, minimal amount of honey or brown sugar, oil or butter.	Cookies where major ingredients (first listed) are sugar, shortening, bleached flour.
CORN MEAL	Yellow, undegermed, ground from whole corn.	Degerminated corn meal.

CRACKERS	Made from whole grains or flours; no shortening, or sugar: Allgrane Wafers, Ideal Flat Bread, Finn Crisp, Wasa Swedish Crisp Bread, Wasa Ry-King.	
DRIED PEAS, BEANS AND LENTILS	Buy a wide variety, use often. Eat with milk, cheese, meat, or cereals.	
FISH, SHELLFISH	Fresh, frozen, canned. All kinds.	Breaded fish and shellfish. Dyed smoked fish.
FLAVORINGS	Pure extracts.	Imitation flavorings.
FRUITS AND VEGETABLES	All kinds.	Wilted, old produce.
GINGER ROOT, FRESH	Look in Oriental, Spanish, and Middle Eastern stores. Store in freezer.	
GRAINS	See individual names.	Don't buy, or cook with, rancid grains and flours.
ICE CREAM	Buy good quality. "Honey" ice cream does not necessarily mean "no sugar."	Artificially flavored kinds. "Strawberry ice cream" for instance, must be made with real fruit. "Strawberry-flavored" is artificially flavored.
JAMS, JELLIES, PRESERVES	Use in moderation. "Made with honey" does not necessarily mean "made without sugar."	

MALT SYRUP	Hop-flavored; excellent in rye bread.	
MAPLE PRODUCTS	Delicious but expensive; no special nutritional values.	Syrup from trees treated with formaldehyde (check label). Maple- *flavored* syrup, etc.
MILK	Use fresh, canned, and dried; pasteurized, and fortified with vitamins A and D. Goats milk okay, but tastes "goatey."	Milk in clear glass or white plastic bottles; loss of riboflavin is rapid in light. Uncertified raw milk.
MILLET	Whole hulled. Flour.	
MOLASSES	Buy unsulphured; blackstrap, dark or light.	
NUTS	All kinds. Preferably unroasted. Shelled, or in shell.	
OATS	Flour. Groats. *Steel cut. Rolled.*	
OILS, SALAD AND COOKING	Try one kind one time, a different one the next. Corn germ, sesame, safflower, soybean, avocado, olive, etc. Once opened, store in refrigerator; do not use rancid oils.	
PASTA	Preferably whole wheat or buckwheat. Soba noodles. Bean thread noodles.	

PEANUT BUTTER	Made from peanuts only, with or without salt. Added wheat germ okay.	
RICE	*Natural brown.* Brown rice cream. Rice polishings (use like wheat germ). Converted white rice second choice to brown.	
RYE	*Cracked. Flour.* Grits. Meal.	
SALT	Kosher salt. Or iodized salt with minimum of extra additives. Sea salt has little extra to offer, if anything.	
SALAMI AND SIMILAR PRODUCTS	Eat only occasionally, high in fat.	Beef jerky and similar products.
SEAWEED	Laver (nori), hiziki (kelp) and dulse are the most useful.	
SEEDS	Fresh, raw, pumpkin and sunflower. Unhulled sesame. Alfalfa and others for sprouting.	
SNACK PRODUCTS	Fresh and dried fruits; vegetables, nuts, seeds; cheese, yogurt, whole-grain cookies and crackers.	Potato chips, corn chips, and all similar fried snacks. Pretzels. Most packaged cakes, pies, cookies, etc. Puddings and gels.
SORGHUM SYRUP	Dark syrup made from a cereal grass.	

SOYBEAN PRODUCTS	Powder or flour for bread and cakes. Tofu (bean curd). Miso (fermented bean paste). Grits, granules, fresh and dried soybeans. Beverage and "milk" powders.	
SUGAR, TURBINADO		No better than regular brown sugar.
SYRUPS	Use real maple and sorghum syrups, or honey or molasses.	
VINEGAR	Cider, rice, wine. Herb-flavored vinegars.	
WHEAT	*Wheat kernels* for sprouting. Unbromated, stone ground *whole-wheat flour* (unbolted, graham, or 80 percent extraction). Whole-wheat pastry flour. Bran flakes (use like wheat germ). *Wheat germ,* (vacuum packed, raw).	
YEAST, BREWERS	Add in small amounts to stews, breads, soups.	
YEAST, BAKERS	Dried, or compressed fresh.	
YOGURT	Plain. Made from whole milk, or part skim.	Yogurt made with carrageen, gelatin, guar gum, dextrose (a sugar), cornstarch, preservatives, sugary preserves, etc.

11

Mail-Order Sources

All sources will send catalogues with prices, except as noted. "O.G." indicates products said to be organically grown.

Briggs-Way Company
Ugashik, Alaska 99683

Alaska salmon canned in glass, with or without salt.

Covalda Date Co.
51–392 Highway 86
Coachella, Calif. 92236

Dates, dried apricots, apples, figs, raisins, walnuts, pecans. O.G. dates

Jaffee Bros.
28560 Lilac Road
Valley Center, Calif. 92082

Seeds, seed and nut butters, honey, juices, salad oils, soy beans, dried fruits, dates, nuts. Most O.G.

Sierra Natural Foods
2408 26th Street
Sacramento, Calif. 95818

Dates, figs, prunes, raisins, dried apricots and peaches; almonds, walnuts, black walnuts. O.G.

Sioux Millers
RR 1, Whiting
Iowa 51063

Full line of products but tops in grains and freshly ground flours. Many O.G., including soybeans.

Donn's Health Foods
14 Oak Street
Lisbon Falls, Maine

No catalogue. Full line of grains, seeds, fruits, nuts, etc.

Richard's Natural Food Farm Hinman Road Eagle, Michigan 48822	Organically grown whole wheat, rye, soybeans, and white hull-less popcorn.
Seppanen's Natural Foods Farm Store Route 3 Alexandria, Minn. 56308	Freshly ground flours. Grains, seeds, dried fruits, nuts, oils. Much O.G. (Organically raised beef—but *not* by mail)
Deer Valley Farm Guilford, N.Y.	Everything. Most O.G.
Thousand Island Apiaries Clayton, N.Y. 13624	Liquid, creamed, and comb honey.
Alexander's Health Food Shop 278 South Main Street Akron, Ohio 44308	Grains, seeds, honey, herb teas, nuts, nut butters.
L. & L. Health Foods Company Route 1, Box 197 Fairview, Oklahoma 73737	Good on grains, also seeds, peanut butter, dried fruits, oils. Some O.G.
Better Foods Foundation Inc. Box 9 North Washington Street Greencastle, Pennsylvania 17225	Nuts, seeds, cereals, grains. Some O.G.
Walnut Acres Penns Creek Pennsylvania 17862	Organically grown items clearly marked.
Arrowhead Mills, Inc. Box 866 Hereford, Texas 79045	300-pound minimum order, but top source for organically grown peanuts, grains, beans. Share order with friends.
Champlain Valley Apiaries Box 127, Middlebury Vermont 05753	Liquid or crystallized honey.
Tweedmeadow Stockbridge, Vermont 05772	Maple syrup, honey, flours, grains, seeds, dried fruits, oil, herb teas.
Essential Foods Co.	Fresh ground rye and wheat flours

2023 W. Wisconsin Avenue
Milwaukee, Wisconsin 53233

shipped regularly—on contract if you wish. O.G.

Hickory Hill Farm
Loganville, Wisconsin 53943

Whole grains, fresh ground flours, nuts, seeds, cereals, honey, cheese. Much O.G.

Leon R. Horsted
Route 2
Waunakee, Wisconsin 53597

Flours from organically grown grains. Dill pickles, maple syrup, sunflower kernels, sauerkraut, raw peanuts.

Western Natural Foods Co.
1334 Second Avenue
Seattle, Washington

Seeds, nuts, grains, dried fruits. No catalogue. Ship to Alaska and West Coast only.

Index